"GOOD-BY1

My Work

*This is my statement of beliefs that I seek to hold as my
constant companion.*

*I believe my thoughts are the trigger to all that I
experience, and how I interpret what I experience
determines my form.*

*I am the result of my thoughts. Everything in my
reciprocating world begins with a thought, and so
for peace in my life, I endeavour hard to abstain
from thoughts of harm toward others.*

*The more I practise this abstention, and the more I reach
out to others, the more I reap incalculable returns
when I least expect them.*

*When stymied at life's crossroads, I believe that to seek
the path that aligns me with the purpose of the
Higher Force will create harmony at the deepest
level, and lead me to my destiny.*

*The true purpose of the Higher Force is to inspire and
give certitude, a feeling of absolute certainty
necessary in nurturing my creative talents.*

*Therefore, when I inspire others, I believe I am letting
the Higher Force act through me as its instrument.*

*To strive not to take credit for any such deeds, and to
put the glory of such deeds in the lap of the Higher
Force is an act of supreme humility.*

I believe that my truest sense of liberation from the shackles of social conditioning will come when I am totally free of judgment, and when I accept everything without condemning.

I believe that only when I am free of judgment and prejudice, only when race, religion, gender, status, titles, accumulations and all descriptions become secondary to my true purpose in life, will I begin to experience the Divine and manifest my destiny.

I believe that there are no bad or evil human beings, only prisoners of warped thinking.

These distinctions will cease to be when these fellow beings board my bus of life to journey into the infinite inner world.

I believe that to strive to amass wealth is not immoral, but it is a form of lust when it ceases to be a goal and becomes a purpose, a perpetual grind, in life.

Accumulated wealth is a myth; until it is put to use for general and common good, it is not true wealth, only a burdensome yoke.

I believe that man does not need religion to experience God; the real truth is that which I have uncovered for myself, and not that which is thrust upon me.

The higher truth, though, is that there is no real point in holding vehemently on to such truths, for yesterday's truth is today not what it was, and tomorrow will bring another superseding truth.

*I strive to remain open-minded and let the mysteries of
life continue to bewilder me.*

*I believe that to see a good hidden purpose or joy and
glory in all events of existence and in every
circumstance is the truest form of expression of
gratitude.*

*Behind every event the intelligent Higher Force has a
purposeful hand, and to credit it with all that
happens in my world is the beginning of true
emancipation the beginning of the need not to
possess anything, or be anyone other than my true
self.*

Anil Kumar

Contents

ONE

"GOOD-BYE, MR. PATEL"

"You were born with potential.
You were born with goodness and trust.
You were born with ideals and dreams.
You were born with greatness.
You were born with wings.
You are not meant for crawling, so don't.
You have wings.
Learn to use them and fly"

Rumi. 13th century

"I am very sorry Mr. Patel, but there is no scholarship for you." He looked up and continued, *"You will have to make other arrangements to pay your fees."* These chilling words, which momentarily meant the end of the world, will always remain with me. They changed the entire course of my life, and with that, my outlook on life.

As I look back I realise that the severe wounds dealt on my psyche by these words have taken decades to heal. I state at the outset that this is not a reflection on the person who spoke them, but rather on the extent of my sensitivity to the harshness and cruelty behind words spoken by people supposedly in positions of power and influence. I have now, for a long time, discerned in me an ongoing process of self-healing, purification and cleansing that started in the aftermath of that event. It has contributed vastly to my spiritual and psychological growth. I have come a long way and, whilst not claiming to be a writer by any stretch of imagination, I wish to share the constructive experiences of my journey so far with all the readers of this work, particularly young individuals striving to find a purpose and a sense of achievement in life.

The chilling words were spoken by the principal of the College of Commerce in Kampala, Uganda, in May 1967, and meant that I had to leave the college instantly, after being there for only one term. Several years of hard work and yearning came to an abrupt end. I felt as if I had been branded as no good and unworthy.

There were no good-byes. My college friends did not know what had happened, except that they were bemused by my silence as I gathered my meagre books and clothes, and set off unceremoniously for home, feeling ashamed and bitter. The journey back that day was very painful and seemed like an eternally long one. Disappointment and sadness had choked me.

I kept repeating to myself, *don't give up - you must keep your hopes alive,* as I continued striding, rucksack on my back. I must have walked on the roadside, in the sweltering equatorial sun, for more than two hours before realising that I should have been hitching for a lift.

Soon I was seated in the back of a lorry that was bound for my hometown, Mbale, more than a hundred miles away. I had ample time to reflect, not only on the events of that morning, but also on the nineteen years of my life then. In spite of my very humble upbringing and all the associated harsh experiences of the childhood struggles, I felt the greatest amount of humiliation on that day.

I did not want to go home. *How will Ba take this?* My greatest worry was my mother. *How will she take the news of the premature end to my academic life, especially after all the sacrifices and hard work put into my education by herself and my elder brother and sister?*

Their expectations of me were high, and they looked forward to the day I would qualify as a certified accountant, the highest accountancy qualification attainable in Uganda by attending college. A formal qualification meant a great deal in those days, mainly because it was seen as the gateway to happiness. Society looked up to you. You would certainly have a job, respectable enough to attract prospective in-laws in search of a good home and an educated husband for their daughter. To my family, my degree would not only be a matter of great pride, but also a smack in the face of those relatives and close acquaintances who distanced themselves from us soon after my father's death, obviously fearing we would land on their doorstep for shelter, and also a smack in the face of those who looked down on us - a mother and six children. They ridiculed us, during our time of great hardship, for trying to do the impossible, that is to make a life in Africa without a father instead of going back to India. Poverty attracts a subtle kind of cruelty from one's own kind but on the other hand it does make one strong with resolve.

It was customary, according to my mother, to have large families in those days in Africa because of a high mortality rate amongst children. More than fifty percent of children died before they were ten. Fortunately, thanks to my mother's resourcefulness, we all survived our infancies.

For the first time in my life I had gone down on my knees that morning and begged for that scholarship. The award was from the Madhvani Trust, to be given to the most deserving students but at the final discretion of the college principal. Good academic performance and pecuniary difficulties generally dictated the case for the most deserving candidates. I felt I was safe on these grounds, until I heard the principal say, "*I have chosen to give the award to a more deserving African student.*" An African being given scholarship was laudable, but not at my expense. My outstanding Senior Cambridge examination results did not carry any weight as far as he was concerned. Senior Cambridge examinations were set by a UK education body in those days and were a matter of great pride for all those who passed them. "*I have worked hard for this scholarship, Sir. Without it my career will come to an end,*" I pleaded, and continued in humiliation, "*I come from a family with limited means. My family cannot afford my college education. I have no relatives or guardians I can turn to.*" He was unmoved, as he said disdainfully, "*Surely you can go to one of your rich Patel brothers who will help you with money, Mr. Patel.*" Seeing that I was distraught, he added, "*It is not the end of the world you know, old chap. We all have to face difficult situations in life at one time or the other. I don't want you to lose hope.*" I was not impressed. In desperate moments, man's emotions take over. I stood up and retorted most uncharacteristically, "*But Sir, late Mr. Madhvani was an Indian, if not a Patel, at least a Gujarati like me.*" The late Mr. Muljibhai Madhvani was a prominent, philanthropic, highly admired, respected and very successful industrialist in Uganda. The principal listened as I continued, charged with emotion, "*It seems to me, Sir, that an African is being given the scholarship for being an African, and I am being denied it for being a Patel.*" It was unheard of for good students like me to ever stand up to any member of the teaching profession. A teacher was regarded as the pillar of the society. He removed his spectacles and peered at me for a few seconds before lashing out, "*I am aware of late Mr. Madhvani's background, and in case you haven't noticed, I am an Indian myself. Thank you for insulting my intelligence,*" he continued, "*I am talking about Patels, you Patels,*" he pointed his demeaning index finger at me, "*I want you to find one of your Patel brothers to help you. They have lots of money.*" The wry smile on his face disappeared as he continued, "*Instead of spending it on flamboyant weddings and lavish parties and hiving off what has remained to England, I am sure they can show some mercy towards causes like you.*"

He put on his glasses and leaned back. I was left speechless, in tears, and trembling. This was the worst moment of my life. As there was no more left to say, I turned and left his office. There was an expression of total indifference on his face. I had not experienced such contempt previously. I was too young to appreciate the politics or self-interest or any other force behind his decision, but it was evident that he did not think very highly of Patels.

As I look back on this episode, now several decades later, I am convinced he was a very insecure man who was struggling to survive in the post-independence Ugandan-African administration. Possibly in his quest to gain favour with the Administration he made me his victim. I was an easy target for this man who did not have a backbone. Life has taught me that weak people put in position of power can often be devastatingly dangerous - they are driven by self-interest only, not any sense of rectitude. They show little conviction of any kind, and so have no need for courage or strength. They are low in spirit but thrive on exerting mastery over those who are underprivileged and helpless.

Soon after I arrived home and narrated the events of the day to my family, the neighbourhood became aware of it all. There was general silence at home. Everyone received the news with awe and dismay. There was no discussion about the principal; no harsh words were uttered by anyone. We all knew deep within that I did not deserve such a setback.

It was not long before there was a knock on the front door of my house that evening. My younger sister let in the headmaster of a privately owned local secondary school who lived in the neighbourhood. He came straight to the point after saying some encouraging words. He wanted me to help with teaching mathematics at his school until some decision was taken about my future. I was commanded to appear at the school the following morning. I would be paid a small salary, enough for a single person to live on.

This was an amazing turn of events. In less than twelve hours, I was fit enough to teach at a secondary school in my own town! I can say in retrospect that everything in life happens for the best. What was unfolding was just beyond imagination. The word went round the neighbourhood like wild fire. I felt at least there was some recompense for the humiliation I had suffered that morning. I would be able to face the community in my new capacity. My pride was restored to some extent.

The next few months that followed were calm, purposeless and uneventful; I was drifting without volition. There was a real danger that I would reconcile myself with being a junior unqualified teacher. Life at home was exceptionally quiet. Somehow I could sense deep discontent and frustration. Nobody, particularly my elder brother, spoke about what I should be doing next.

I shared their feelings, but had begun to put into

practice subconsciously what I had been taught by life; *when your best endeavours to attain a goal have failed, say what you want and let go of the desire for it.* Let nature take its course. What then happens always happens for the best. In my own way, I was truly beginning to leave things to the Higher Spirit, or Nature as many would prefer to call it. Over a period of months my thoughts and desire to gain some kind of professional qualification had transformed into a kind of contemplation. Contemplation, as opposed to meditation, is a wonderful state of mind under which earnest desires make a lasting home in one's thoughts, and finally become a part of one's consciousness. Thereafter, it is only a matter of time before the desired results begin to manifest themselves.

Later that year I was selected to play my first ever representative cricket match in the annual National Pentangular Tournament. Five teams were selected from five major cricket playing ethnic groups in the country; that is Indians, Muslims, Goans, Europeans and Africans. Cricket was a major sport in the country. The national team was always selected on the basis of the performance of each individual participant in this tournament. I was the youngest player in my ethnic team selected to play against the Europeans at the Lugogo stadium in Kampala, the capital city of Uganda. This was the national stadium where all important cricket fixtures were staged. The other players in my team did not have much to say, except to perfunctorily congratulate and welcome the young debutant to the team. I was naturally nervous, and a little apprehensive. I did not know how I was going to fare. I found the atmosphere in the team rather tense, and clearly not enjoyable. Every player was concerned about his own performance because of the importance attached to this match. There were no friends in the team. Everyone was vying for a place in the national squad to play against the visiting Mick Stewart XI from England under the auspices of the MCC. I felt lonely and chose to remain quiet. Upon the fall of the second wicket, as I stood up to go out to bat, the captain, who was an austere man, wished me luck. On stepping out of the pavilion on to the field, I realised, to my utter astonishment that a large group of spectators was waiting for me to emerge. I was given a rapturous reception by a crowd of several thousand cricket enthusiasts. I was the boy they had been looking forward to seeing in the provincial and the national teams for more than two years. My performances in the national inter-school competitions and inter-town league had been noticed by all. Having been the youngest debutant for my town team, Elgon Rovers, at the age of fourteen, I had already made a name for myself. This was largely due to courage and coaching given by my science teacher and cricket master, C. C. Patel, who became a close friend later in life.

Teachers played an important part in our lives in those days. My elder brother, Manhar, who was my biggest cricket fan and supporter, played a major part in all this too. He was truly proud of all my achievements. Notwithstanding my early successes on the cricket pitch though, I had not been allowed to make myself available for any representative cricket until now because of critical examinations. Education always came first, and I had been working for that scholarship which of course did not materialise. Here I was now on the first big cricketing day of my life with no worries about examinations.

Those who have the chance to experience this kind of situation will easily appreciate what I mean when I say that as I approached the wicket to take guard, there was an all-round silence that can only be described as deathly or deafening - the spectators and fielders waiting in anticipation. This silence was noticeable and extremely loud inside me. I could hear my own breath during these awesome opening moments. Being the only boy on the field against eleven big looking Englishmen, I was nervous and my lips were dry. In those days we saw the

English, being the colonial masters, as superior and very powerful.

Hands trembling, I stooped to pick up the piece of chalk from behind the stumps to mark my guard on the matting whilst the fielding captain was having a momentary discussion with the bowler. They set the field after planning their strategy on how they should get me out. The wicket keeper, Stan Bowles, who knew me from previous encounters at club level, was standing up. The piece of chalk fell from my hand. Stan kindly handed it back to me. Noticing my extreme nervousness, he uttered, *"How's life?"* *"Very boring"*, I muttered and then proceeded to ask the umpire to check middle and leg. He did not understand the words from my mouth and asked me to repeat my request. I did and was set to take strike.

It was noticeable that the fielding side waited patiently until I was ready. Stan patted me on the back with a gloved hand and muttered, *"Good luck, old chap"*; a most unusual gesture, as if I was someone special, which was noticed by everyone. All the nervousness dissipated in a moment.

The bowler, whose name I cannot remember, was a tall bespectacled medium pacer who ran up and delivered an out-swinger just wide of the off stump. I leaned forward and drove the ball on the rise through the cover area and didn't even bother to run knowing full well that the ball would reach the boundary. For any batsman to drive the ball off the front foot whilst it is still rising is a difficult, but a very attractive, shot to play. *"Great shot!"* Stan shouted from behind in a tone of veritable admiration. The crowd erupted. I was away.

On reflection, I now appreciate that Stan's encouraging remarks were a kind and sporting gesture of the highest order - indeed he put my interest ahead of his team's and therefore at that moment he actually elevated himself to a higher level of existence - a spiritual level of existence. At that level he was able to raise my spirit, and thus his own too. Spirituality exists every fraction of a second in every walk of life. It is a state of existence in which one is replete with a clear sense that there is a divine force present in every breath that every individual takes. Each act that such a person performs places a human being first and foremost at the very centre of that action - human emotions and feelings matter most to such individuals. For Stan, winning or losing was secondary to admiring and encouraging a young talent out in the colonies.

Over the ensuing twenty exhilarating years of cricket at various levels, as a player, captain, coach and manager, I learnt to practise what Stan taught me in one short moment on that day - that is to understand, encourage and motivate young talent - and I can say with pride that it brought me friendship and respect. I am most grateful to Stan. I have no hesitation to say that Stan was a worthy representative of the British Government in Uganda, a credit to the Empire.

Each and every one of us is gifted with what I call a natural receiver and a transmitter inside us. With these instruments we are able to maintain connectedness with the forces of Nature and all other minds. My receiver was telling me, *'It's your day, old boy. You are in charge'*. I was completely at ease with myself and deep down I felt invincible. Indeed it must have been the will of all the well-wishers present on the day that I should excel, and sure enough their will prevailed. I rose to the occasion, thrilled the crowd with an array of uninhibited strokes and played a big match-winning innings and remained not out.

It has to be believed that Nature works in wonderful ways. The day was not over yet. That evening I was seated alone outside the players' changing room, waiting for transport to arrive, when a girl, about ten years old, approached me and asked, *"Are you Anil Patel?"* I replied in the affirmative. She placed an envelope beside me and hurriedly walked away. I did not open it immediately, thinking that it was possibly another congratulatory message from some kind admirer.

However, moments later, when I opened the envelope, I found to my amazement that it contained money - hard cash. I held it in my hand and momentarily gazed at it absolutely dumbfounded. The amount of money - in the form of notes - in my hand was unimaginable. It was customary in Uganda for spectators to reward players with instant cash, often during play, to show appreciation, but this was usually in small amounts. The money I held in my hand that evening was not a small amount. I recognised several large denomination notes, and not wanting to attract attention, instantly put it all in my pocket. The little girl was gone. I felt terribly frustrated that I did not take a good look at her, or even thank her.

Later that evening I counted the money and found that suddenly, taking into account my meagre savings and what my elder brother was able to offer me, I was the proud owner of sufficient wealth to pay for a ticket to fly to London, buy some clothes and live on in London for a few weeks! With help and encouragement from the family, I was soon on my way to gain a professional qualification in the UK.

Deep down in my heart, and in my contemplation, this was what I had always wanted; to become a UK qualified chartered accountant because this was the only internationally recognised professional qualification I could attain without the need to be financially supported. Secondly, the memory of my father as a well-respected Mbale branch manager of an accountancy practice in Uganda had, to a certain extent, influenced me to follow this profession. He was not a qualified accountant but rather a self-made man who learnt and progressed from working with other people. He managed books and accounts of varying businesses and trades. Not being qualified, he could not certify accounts but otherwise he was, for all intents and purposes, relied upon by his employer to do all the work necessary to bring accounts to a certifiable state. He was passionate about his firm's clients' affairs and took extreme pride in training new staff in the office.

His office was attached to our house, and consequently he could work long hours without being too far from us. His passion for his work was intense. I recall how excitedly he shared an instance with an office colleague one morning. An erroneous entry in a client's ledger, that he could not detect easily, was causing an imbalance in the accounts. It had been bothering him for several hours and was so much on his mind that he actually discovered the cause of the imbalance in his sleep. He got out of bed that instant, walked to his desk, saw where the error was and immediately put it right before going back to bed. He was truly admired by all who had experience of seeing him at work.

As a prerequisite to becoming a chartered accountant, an aspirant with requisite secondary school education entered into a contract of articleship with a practitioner, a principal, in a UK-based firm of chartered accountants, and earned a small, but adequate, remuneration for being employed to work in the firm and gain practical experience whilst also studying for professional examinations set by an institute given a Royal Charter to run the profession.

As I had no resources for going to England and because I had qualified for a scholarship to study to become a certified accountant in Uganda, I had opted to study in Uganda. The main shortcoming with certified accountancy was that, after passing examinations, one had to gain and demonstrate sound practical experience before being recognised as a professional accountant, whereas a chartered accountant was recognised immediately upon passing the examinations. Moreover, naïve as it may sound, there was an air of superiority - something appealing and self-assuring - in the exaggerated swagger of a few chartered accountants I had met that I was bowled over by.

My brother made arrangements for me to begin life in London. I was to stay with a family who were very close friends of ours, they having emigrated to England from Mbale.

How could anyone believe this turn of events?

Looking back now decades later with an inquiring mind, I believe that this was no luck. This was the creative force working in its characteristic, most magnanimous style to gift me with a means to propel me forward in life.

During the preceding few months when I was teaching, I had genuinely cleansed myself of all the poison inside me that had been created by the experience at the college. There was no bitterness anymore. In reality this was not a deliberate action on my part. It just happened as I took my attention away from the setback. Not only that, but under an inner guidance I had begun to dedicate myself to giving of myself to those pupils who needed help. In return, this had begun to give me a sense of purpose and joy. I had first-hand experience of how it feels when one is denied education. I even took time to give free tuition to our domestic servant who was about my age. Deep within, I was at peace with myself with an assuring optimism about the future. Somehow I felt that something wonderful had to happen in my life. Nature always arrives with the right help in time - to always give is its basic characteristic - only we have to be in harmony with it, be clear deep within about our true intentions and live knowing that it is only a matter of time before fulfilment arrives.

I recollect the words of Henry David Thoreau, "*If you advance confidently in the direction of your dreams and endeavour to live the life you have imagined for yourself, you will meet with success unexpected during common hours.*" To me this comes over as a very powerful statement. When its words are fully understood and taken into one's consciousness without adulteration, blissful and unbridled joy begins to be ushered into one's life from an unfolding sense of success. There are no setbacks in life, only small obstacles so Nature has time to organise and orchestrate the course for one to go forth towards one's destiny.

TWO

London, Great London

One parting gesture from an elderly well-wisher was to remind me that, like Mahatma Gandhi and so many other great Indian men, I now had the privilege of the opportunity to be educated in England. His message was that my only aim should be to return home soon as an upright professional man. Such advice was customary, founded on fear that otherwise I would neglect education, fall in love with and marry an English girl and be a loss to the community. My resolve had clearly not been appreciated. At least there was an element of some well-intentioned advice in what he said.

But my stomach churns when I think of very many other elders who voluntarily took it upon themselves to thrust uninvited cautionary advice and guidance at me without ever attempting to engage in any discussion to know my thoughts and opinions on my career. It was as if upon reaching certain age they had an unquestionable right to impose their will and opinion on the likes of me. One of them, who must have had a very closed mind, did just the opposite in an attempt to dissuade me from going away from home; he actually stated that I would be back home within three months because chartered accountancy was a very difficult career to pursue in England.

Deep within I did not pay any heed to any of this advice simply because not one of them had risen high enough in my esteem to be worthy a counsellor, not one of them truly cared for what happened to me, therefore their words had no strength in them, and I could sense it all. Indeed with one or two of them there was jealousy or a sense of disbelief that I would be going to England for further education when their own children could not.

Coming to England was a major event in my life. In those days I viewed Britain as a distant land where the colonial masters lived and could only be visited by the rich and the privileged. My privilege was that after tens of applications over a number of weeks, I secured one interview which resulted in an offer of articleship. This was most heartening as I could now bury the dreaded thought of returning to Uganda empty handed.

London opened up a whole new world for me. As an articled clerk, looking to better myself, I soon realised the value of public libraries, multiple choices of newspapers, BBC, Speakers Corner in Hyde Park, theatres, public parks, museums and numerous other public places and institutions, not to mention excellent roads, the fascinating London tube trains, the ubiquitous double-decker buses and the unique black taxis. It was safe to go out, alone on foot, any time of the day, as there were lights in all public places and the police were always there to come to your aid. Everything was always well-organised. There were no beggars in the streets, and everyone seemed to have roof over his head. There were no visible signs of any poverty. The streets were immaculately clean. There was a tremendous civic sense on the part of everyone who was immensely proud of the nation. *How can someone take all the trouble to cross a busy street only to put an empty packet of cigarettes in a bin located there and walk back across again?* I would ask myself. This was real civilisation. *No wonder they ruled the world,* I used to say to myself.

The freedom of speech so evident in the country and the opportunity to take charge of my own life without any fear or pressure of the society, made me more confident and self-assured. I seriously began to analyse, in my own crude way, what had transpired to bring me to London. I could not totally forget the incident at the college but started to see it as a stepping stone to better opportunities. My belief in the saying '*whatever happens, happens for the best*' was reinforced. The anonymous donor had restored my faith in the people around me. There is always someone out there who means well. I have no idea who this magnanimous person was but, to this day, I have remembered the generosity and have always personally striven to balance things out by giving to others in whatever manner I can.

I am glad to record that the episode at the college in Uganda did not change my views on any member of the then teaching profession or on how education was administered in Uganda. I was privileged to have been taught by men and women whom I have always held in high esteem. Teachers were always given credit for all successes in life, big or small, attained by their pupils. The reason for this, I presume, was that the teacher generally undertook the unwritten responsibility to attempt to inculcate virtuous qualities in all his pupils. Punishment from a teacher, corporal or otherwise, was always seen as part of constructive and holistic education - meaning that emphasis was always on creating a whole person out of a young life. This emphasis in school, which met with full parental approval, was a great credit to the education system which I can appreciate now, as can everyone at that time. We could not conceive of cases of severe bullying that led to pupils committing suicide, murders of fellow pupils at school, indulgence in drugs, alcohol and toxic substances, threatening behaviour towards teachers and teenage pregnancies. The teacher-pupil relationship was much deeper. Our teachers, some of whom we may have found to be rather idiosyncratic, essentially made it their business to care for our well-being. One day in class, my English teacher came up to me at my desk and turned my shirt collar inside out and took a good look at it. I was embarrassed because I knew it to be slightly worn. Next day I was discreetly presented with a new shirt and all she said was, *"You've done very well. This is a present from me. It's your size. I checked it, remember?"* She was aware of my meagre resources. There was a teacher-pupil connectedness that is difficult to describe. The teachers were not 'teaching subjects' but rather 'educating us'.

Thus, in sports we were taught that more important than winning was the very act of participation and trying one's hardest, enjoying the sport and practising good sportsmanship in a team environment. In cricket, it was every player's duty to make the umpire's job easy through restraint from unnecessary appealing and accepting decisions unreservedly; in fact it was every striking batsman's duty to nod to the umpire in response to an appeal if his bat had touched the ball and every fielder's duty to tell the umpire if the ball had not been caught cleanly. I know of a case where a fielding captain withdrew his appeal and requested the batsman, given run out, to return to the crease upon being told by his boundary fielder that the ball had crossed the line before it was thrown back to the keeper.

Standards in all the schools were seen as meeting the needs of the society. There were no inferior or superior institutions of education. However, because of limited places in the state-owned secondary schools, all pupils were subjected to junior school-leaving examinations. Naturally a number of pupils each year failed to gain entry into these secondary schools. But their parents had the choice to take them to recognised secondary schools set up by private entrepreneurs. It was at such a school that I was a teacher for a while after the episode at the college.

The episode at the college was still hounding me although there was much to get on with in England before returning home as a professional. Why did the college principal have so much contempt for Patels? Was he a fair-minded person? How is a Patel viewed by other Asians? Are Patels imbued with vainglory? In my quest for answers to these and many more questions, I met more Patels in the late nineteen sixties as they started to arrive from East Africa, mainly Kenya. In 1972 they also came in droves from Uganda under Idi Amin's marching orders. This was history in the making.

Asians in East Africa had created an economic and social class that stood out above Africans and other ethnic immigrant and resident minorities. Wealthy Asians were generally seen by Africans as arrogant and indifferent towards them. It had long been evident, to a significant number of them, that Asians had no long-term commitment to Africa. Their loyalties lay with their homeland, primarily either India or Pakistan. In the immediate aftermath of his decision to expel the Asians from Uganda, Amin became very popular amongst the indigenous Ugandans. He did not care to differentiate between citizen and non-citizen Asians, rich and poor, or professionals and others. They were all treated alike; with equal contempt. The marching orders applied to one and all.

All of a sudden, the Asians were dominating the headlines in the UK media. This was yet another blow to my spirit. I wanted to return to Uganda with a good knowledge of commerce gained in an advanced country to help build a strong independent nation I ceased to think like a student seeking academic betterment. In the public eye I was like all other Asians; refugees, immigrants, tourists and students alike. This whole episode was a great equaliser - the rich and the not-so-rich, Hindus, Sikhs, Moslems, Christians, men, women, children; the whole lot subjected to the same public humiliation and ridicule. Many indigenous Britons also suffered a kind of humiliation as they helplessly witnessed planeloads of new arrivals everyday. Nobody could stop the process. These were refugees from a British colony. There was a public uproar for the government to do something about this seemingly unstoppable invasion of an already crowded island. Parliament debated the whole affair vigorously, as did several representatives of the media and public institutions.

A Conservative politician, Enoch Powell, an erudite and articulate orator, stood above all others for his jingoistic condemnation of multiracial immigration into Britain. He has gone down in history as arguably one of the most controversial British politicians of the post-war era. His earlier speeches during the Kenyan exodus had already attracted a great deal of attention. He spoke fearlessly and coherently in his portrayal of 'rivers of blood' that would ensue from an ideologically polarized British society. He believed, and said as much, that English heritage was under threat.

I felt that, by default of Amin's actions, I had now become part of Powell's sordid and alarmist extrapolations of demographic statistics. I was not wanted in Britain. I was made to feel as if I was a burden on the country. In public there was no difference amongst Asian immigrants, refugees, work permit holders, students and visitors. I began to notice distinctly that the characteristic British warmth, to which I had become accustomed, was being gradually eroded and overtaken by indifference towards me.

This was yet another very serious blow to my spirit. My cherished dream of going back to Uganda as a professional person and to live there as though I belonged there was already shattered by Amin, but now Powell's speeches put an end to living and growing in Britain with a true sense of belonging to Britain. I was barely in my twenties when this experience planted long lasting and searching questions in my mind, *"Where do I belong? Can I avoid belonging anywhere? Is it necessary to belong to any nation?"* Whilst harbouring these questions to which there were no immediate answers, I chose to set my mind on what life had to offer then and how I much better I would make my life as a chartered accountant.

As it was, the immigration topic was soon out of the headlines. The Ugandan Asians were absorbed, began to find occupations and started to buy homes. What the East African Asians achieved commercially and materially in the ensuing decades speaks for itself.

THREE

PATELS AND PATELS

It was just before this upheaval in my life that one day, as I boarded a bus on a short four-stop journey from Shepherds Bush to Acton Vale, a certain Gujarati gentleman, a Patel, followed me and took the seat opposite. He greeted me and started to ask personal questions. I obliged him as he was much older than I and, seemingly, his intrusion was simply out of curiosity, which was quite common then amongst the Asian immigrants. Before I reached my destination, he knew that I was from Uganda, unmarried, studying to become a chartered accountant, a Patel from a particular line of descendants and originating from Dharmaj - a village in Gujarat regarded as very rich in culture and wealth. This information was sufficient for him to assess my character, marriage eligibility and strength to command a dowry.

As I stood up to disembark, he whispered, *"Would you like to get married?"* I let out a shy laugh and shook my head. I did not know how else to react. He was unrelenting and asked me several times if I was interested. He even attempted to lure me with the promise of a substantial dowry that would solve all my current financial problems, help me to buy a house and, on qualifying, to start my own business. He was very serious, indeed, about his offer and said he knew the right girl for me. I was so embarrassed that I hopped off the bus well before it came to stop at my destination.

I was not going to allow a stranger to meddle with my life. As I recounted the incident, it irritated me. A value was put on me, based on a two-minute knowledge of my background, nationality and academic standing. And what about the girl I was to marry? She did not appear to matter. Moreover there was an assumption that I would succumb to the temptation of a dowry - symptomatic of a materialistic system.

I have no qualms with arranged marriages, providing they are properly researched and there is an all round goodwill and acceptance, but the concept of a dowry as a precondition to a marriage is evil and most offensive to any sensible, level headed person, especially when the groom's parents change their mind and increase their demand at a late stage of the wedding preparations. Amongst many communities demand of the dowry continues beyond marriage into birth of children. Weak-minded unprincipled men marry for possessions. For them the dowry system is a shortcut to riches. For parents a son's marriage is an opportunity to acquire possessions in their home which otherwise they cannot afford.

This practice of dowry amongst Indians, albeit now frowned upon widely in India and made illegal there under the Dowry Prohibition Act of 1961, is rooted in the age-old traditions of a nation renowned for being rich in culture. Despite the Act the practice continues unabated. I am certain it had good, practical socio-economic reasons in the past and was probably not abused. Now, this relic of the past suits only, if at all, marriages amongst the rich, who see flamboyant weddings as opportunities to flaunt their wealth. Why should the fathers of grooms in the middle and lower wealth groups imitate the rich and make preposterous demands on families with which they are joining hands in a lasting bondage? It is little wonder that amongst many families in the poorer groups, the marriage of a girl is a burden on her family; in fact the very birth of a girl is seen as a curse. Even now in 'modern' times many women die or are killed in parts of India for disputes and distress over dowry.

Be all that as it may, why should such a tradition be allowed to remain an unshakeable cultural adherent in the western world where I had now made a home? I say this as a person of Indian extract who has not lived in India but was brought up to believe - quite wrongly I hasten to add - that India is my homeland and I will have to return to it one day. In India I would be as much a foreigner as in Africa.

This tradition of dowry has to go. But who am I to change the society? I thought deep and hard about this age-old, deeply entrenched and unshakeable custom. *I can change my own self though.* I made a resolution that my marriage would not be a flamboyant and vulgar exhibition of wealth, no matter how well qualified I was or how rich my in-laws were. It would not be a burden on anyone. I would not stoop to the temptation of easy money from my would-be bride's family, even if I had to subsequently succumb to compromising my beliefs for the sake of getting my sisters married.

There still remained the matter of being pre-judged as a superior class Patel because of my rich, land-owning ancestors, who, for reasons of economic and social well being, built close ties with the Patels in the neighbouring villages in Gujarat, India. For genealogical reasons, each village having been started by one family only, marrying anyone within one's own village is discouraged. Consequently, further close ties were forged with the neighbouring villages through marriages of descendants. Thus, there was a class of rich farming Patels who formed a union of villages which discouraged marriages outside the union, presumably for sentimental reasons, and also to ensure that the wealth given away in dowry remained within the confines of the union. Simultaneously, similar unions were formed by Patels in other parts of Gujarat. However, there were disparities in the total amount of wealth and other natural resources at the disposal of each union. This ultimately resulted in minor cultural differences and gave rise to a hierarchical or class order amongst the Patels, who are all farmers traditionally.

The custom of marrying a Patel within one's own union has continued since then, even when there are no discernible cultural or wealth differences and even when one has never, or rarely, been to one's ancestral village in many cases, like me. Nonetheless, coming from such a centuries-old structured background of clanship, Patels boast culturally rich, homogeneous groups, all falling under one broad umbrella - except for those who may have adopted the name 'Patel' for various practical reasons. Amongst such communities, the system of arranged marriages has a secure home. There is nothing wrong with adhering to one's own clan, but marrying within a clan is not a prerequisite for a happy and successful marriage. I was brought up to believe by my community that Patels of other clans are inferior culturally and I should only marry one of my own clan. Customs and traditions in the right place and at the right time, if observed sensibly and allowed to evolve with changing circumstances, undoubtedly have immense merit in preserving order at community level.

Having been born and raised in East Africa with all kinds of Patels, I could not accept being branded as significantly culturally different, be it superior or inferior, to any other Hindu Patel living outside India. In England, I was an immigrant, probably called by various derogatory terms behind my back. Irrespective of how rich my culture may have been, I, like any other immigrant, was on the lowest rung of the social ladder.

I had to break loose from some of the unworkable cultural shackles, not for reasons of vanity, but to be able to see my new environment objectively and with clarity. Man by nature is territorial; I wanted to extend my boundaries to include other cultures and feel connected with people regarded as different and more distant and incompatible. This kind of thinking was scary and I did not dare to reveal my thoughts to anyone for fear of being ridiculed or admonished. Was I a special creature created by God as a superior being, and did I have to be proud of my heritage as if there was none like it? I convinced myself that the only course open to me was to break away from the shackles of this limiting thought process. I had to distance myself from my old model.

So one day in 1971, I walked into a firm of solicitors and, by a deed poll, shortened my name from Anilkumar Hirabhai Patel to Anil Kumar. I was now Mr. Kumar. Kumar as a surname of a Gujarati is nondescript. It does not say anything about the bearer. As I relocated away from London to Luton and made new acquaintances, I discovered that I was an enigma; someone who spoke and behaved like a Gujarati but did not bear a fitting name. This was what I wanted, not to be taken and judged at face value. To know more about me, it was now necessary for anyone interested to come close enough to me, and be special and respectful enough for me to open up to.

When I qualified, I was Anil Kumar ACA, working for a City firm of accountants, a matter of great pride for all in the family, but many relations, friends and acquaintances thought A. H. Patel, ACA, would have been even better, especially for the community - the very community that was despised in Uganda for being rich,

arrogant and flamboyant. I distinctly recall a wealthy
Patel, from my town in Uganda, once telling me at a
small gathering that by the time I qualified as a chartered
accountant I would be an old man; meaning passing
professional examinations would not be easy for me -
presumably because of my meagre resources and
humble upbringing. I have always resented such cruelty.
It is no wonder that many stalwarts of my clan mistook
me as a misguided arrogant Patel who did not respect
the elders and the old values. This was painful,
particularly because I could not explain that my actions
were guided by past experiences and a burning desire to
explore the world beyond the confines of my inherited
identity. This was necessary if I was to make a real
progress in my new home country and become accepted
as a useful member of the British accountancy
profession.

I do comprehend now, at a very mature stage of my
life, that my past fortunately guided me rather than held
me back. It is worth noting for any reader that past is
gone, it is spent, it has no engine in it to drive us forward,
it merely shows the path we trod and we must not use it
to justify any shortcomings in the present. The result of
not doing this is tantamount to putting our life on a
treadmill that burns us out but takes us nowhere.

The day my wife and I were pronounced married by the registrar with the words, *"Congratulations, I now pronounce you Mr. and Mrs. Kumar"*, some of my wife's relations were rather surprised. Afterwards her paternal uncle asked me, rather inquisitively, *"So, what is this Kumar business?"* When I explained to him that I had shortened my name, his reaction was, *"And what will your children be called?"* I explained that when they grow up they will be told all about it, and they will have the option to choose the surname they prefer. The matter rested there. I have not heard anymore since then.

Incidentally, I chose my bride to whom I was introduced and she turned out to be from a family that my mother would have approved of. There was emphatically no dowry, and the celebrations were kept deliberately simple. Somehow the thought of glamorised marriages has never appealed to me. Marriage is a resolution, witnessed by family and friends, between two consenting individuals to live together and procreate. Therefore how flamboyant or glamorous a wedding is adds no value to the strength of the resolution nor does it confer a happy longevity to the union of the two individuals.

The irony that in modern times the freshness of the memory of regal pomp and ceremony and disproportionate extravagance on the choice of venue, food, drinks, clothing, photography, videos and the rest, in the minds of numerous invitees, outlasts the marriage itself is a sad affair, and is a testimony to the irrelevance of the Bollywood style extravagance to the efficacy of marriage.

In my case it transpired later that I did not have to pay any dowry for my sisters. It was pleasing to know that there were others who thought and acted like me. What is of great merit is not that there were others whose thinking matched mine in the matter of marriage and dowry, but that I was able to attract such individuals into my life. This was a desire rooted in my subconscious. The age-old law of attraction in the world of thought stipulates that a strong and intense thought sustained in one's subconscious for a length of time manifests matching circumstances.

To quote here the words of William Walker Atkinson, the editor of a New York magazine 'The New Thought' in 1901 would seem quite appropriate: *We are sending out thoughts of greater or less intensity all the time, and we are reaping the results of such thoughts. Not only do our thought waves influence ourselves and others, but they have a drawing power – they attract to us the thoughts of others, things, circumstances, people and luck, in accord with the character of the thought uppermost in our minds. Thoughts of love will attract to us the love of others; circumstances and surroundings in accord with the thought; people who are of like thought..."*

Everything begins with a thought, and our thoughts make us *"as you think, so shall you be"*. I wish I had come across and understood the law of attraction in my twenties rather than in my fifties.

FOUR

NEW LIFE, NEW PARADIGMS

I came out alone on my way to my tryst.
But who is this me in the dark?
I move aside to avoid his presence,
but I escape him not.
He makes the dust rise from
the earth with his swagger;
He adds his loud voice
to every word I utter.
He is my own little self, my lord,
he knows no shame;
But I am ashamed to come
to thy door in his company"

Rabindarnath Tagore

So I made a couple of earth shattering statements to my community and friends by altering my surname and having my own way on the matter of dowry. I was riddled though with doubts about my actions and beliefs. What if my path were completely wrong? Only the future would tell. But by then it would be too late to do anything about it. As I reflected on my actions then, I felt deep down that I was perhaps being arrogant. What do I want from life? *What is wrong with my heritage? I am no one special. I am simply being carried away with youthful exuberance.* I would often go into an inward revolving spiral of deep negative thought and become self-critical. *You can never be sure of yourself. There is always someone who knows you better than you. You are young, immature, inexperienced and lack the basic wisdom. Others who are more privileged know best. You don't stand a chance. Society will laugh at you. You will be ridiculed. Your ego needs to be controlled. You are seeking attention.*

This internal dialogue often used to grip me. I didn't think I had the backbone to stand up for myself. I was deeply scripted by the social environment in which I was brought up. There were always the wise elders and the better-placed stalwarts of the community who would decide what was best for me. What friends, acquaintances and groups of people thought and said mattered more than what I wanted for myself from life. In fact I was almost dependant on the approvals of others. What others thought and said was right.

This mental culture was so deeply rooted in me that it could not be simply obliterated by a couple of bold measures. There were stereotypical and unexplained arcane social and communal rights and wrongs from which, I feared, it was not easy to depart. The price for a contrary stand on anything for a youth was exclusion from being included or being boycotted, reprimanded, ridiculed or made the subject of idle gossip. There are subtle ways in which one can be ignored by others, and there is nothing one can do to correct feelings and opinions of others, except to fall into line. Such a stifling mental constitution is an unfortunate by-product of being raised in an insular and self-protective community which lived by an entrenched order and in which everyone was under the watchful eye of everyone else. I was not independent of the opinions of others.

I had to take a good look at myself and what was happening around me. One thing was certain, as time passed, I noticed no one had ridiculed me nor disapproved of what I stood for. In reality no-one, here in England, cared what I stood for. My fears were groundless. If I truly wanted to author my own destiny, there was freedom to do so. Only I had to pluck the courage to act and be accountable for my actions.

What justification was there for all this anyway? Did I need justification for changing my surname? If I did, it was probably only to satisfy myself. This accountability thing was hounding me. There has to be a reason, a justifiable one, for all one's actions. There is a mechanism inside each one of us that dictates and guides our actions. It is a matter of plugging into this mechanism, the voice that speaks from deep down, from the bowels of the conscience.

My search continued until I realised that all I was seeking was freedom from the shackles of social and psychological order surrounding me. I detected imperfections and injustice in my environment. Active mental retention of my early experiences was hindering me, or rather failing to propel me in the right direction. In reality I was lacking conviction and self-belief. There was too much doubt and fear stopping me from taking a leap into a whole new world, a world in which I would be an entity in my own right, propelled by my own beliefs and convictions.

However, it was only a matter of time before my psyche would receive a fillip. Although I was a keen sportsman, one sport I did not admire was boxing. But it is boxing that produced a man who has been one of the few individuals instrumental in bringing about a major transformation in my psychological order.

Cassius Clay, the 1960 Olympic champion, who defeated Sonny Liston in 1964 for the world heavyweight title, became renowned as a man who was fighting the U.S. Administration for his beliefs. It was in the mid-sixties that after becoming the world heavyweight champion, Cassius Clay, an African-American, born a Christian, became a Moslem and changed his name to Mohammed Ali. For his belief, he emphatically refused induction into the U.S. armed forces during the Vietnam conflict, suffered the embarrassment and indignity of a jail sentence and losing his boxing title.

This was a small price to pay to save compromising his integrity and belief. The press and media, mesmerised by Ali's vibrant personality and Islamic message for mankind, never missed an opportunity to give him coverage. He came back to boxing and regained his title. He became a phenomenon, an icon that touched hearts of men. I was certainly moved, not just by his prowess and bold predictions of outcomes in the boxing ring, but also by the strength of conviction and self-belief that dominated his aura. Calling himself the "greatest", Ali came over as a fearless man who saw everything in the clarity and simplicity of divine light. He influenced not just the boxing world but mankind. One commentator wrote of Ali, *There are many men that are affected by times in which they live, but there are very few that actually shape them."*

I found reflecting on Ali a matter of great inspiration. He discovered his true self and found that, for harmony with his attendant consciousness, he needed to stand on a new platform to change the way he viewed his external environment. That meant for him changing religion and his name, and standing proudly by his decision.

The realisation soon came that I needed no justification for my actions. It was inspirational to know that I was sharing this era with Ali whose beliefs were original and forged in the fire of deep agonising questioning in the crucible of his own wretched life conditions.

Whereas these paradigm shifts and psychological changes I chose to undergo caused a great deal of mental trauma and the whole process was riddled with fear and doubt, I can now say that all that was a price worth paying for the inconceivable amount of spiritual growth and inner strength, peace and security it has given me. I thrive on the immense respect and admiration I receive from numerous kind-hearted people.

When we clear our minds of the clutter of useless baggage, worthless information and second-hand knowledge stored to bolster our ego that is allowed to weigh upon us for no discernible reason other than to gain a sense of ascendency over others and to justify our own otherwise meaningless existence, then clear spiritual highways to blissful reality open up.

We realise that the so-called knowledge and information we have gathered from books, media, educators and our surrounding is merely content of our being rather than our essence, the real stuff. Then we realise that what we normally call life is merely an illusory existence which is predicated on the belief that everyone's desired glory, joy and pleasure can only be attained from being bestowed with content, which is used to define, describe and judge an individual.

Therefore content is material possessions, qualifications, character, capabilities, skills, standing in society, accolades, titles, and anything like it that is imputed to the egoist realm. It is this that puts the energy in one's swagger that makes the dust rise from the earth and gives one a feeling of separateness from all. Content is an obstruction on the spiritual highways that blocks the flight beyond the ego where the true inner-self can be experienced.

FIVE

BREAKING THE SHACKLES

It dawned on me that most of my fears, which gave me a sense of inadequacy, were baseless. I was my own worst enemy and a prisoner of my own thinking. In reality I was harbouring a great deal of bitterness about the past events in my life. The baggage from the past was a major hindrance to me. I wish I had known then that the past does not equal the present, nor do any bitter memories of the past propel me forward. What propels me is the energy I create within from inspiring myself.

Inspiration comes from knowing that I have a vast amount of potential locked inside me and only I can galvanise myself to act to fulfil my aims. Nature is very kind, loving and forgiving. It has endowed me with creative mental faculties, a basic sense of right and wrong that points me in the right direction, the freedom to make choices independent of outside influences and the awareness that I can examine my own motives honestly. I can only be grateful to Nature for all this that has been bestowed on me.

It was only when I began to view life with a sense of gratitude and forgiveness that I started to feel at ease with myself and more self-assured. I spent more and more time thinking about my thoughts and consciousness. At first this came to me as an incredible innovation. When one becomes conscious of one's thoughts a realisation comes then that indeed therefore there is a thinker inside – an entity that remains unidentified as long as one allows one's mind to takeover and rule.

My mind becomes hyperactive with a clutter of thoughts which are largely reactions and responses to what I experience daily. I started to go deep within and tried to put aside the effects on my mind of daily occurrences. Thus I began to experience bouts of unexplainable momentary awareness of infinite space within. There were times when I felt that on the inside I was much bigger than I was on the outside. It was the inner world that became my sanctuary during searching moments.

This has been the case with me ever since I realised the value of going inside. The inner is a repository of strength and source of inspiration to handle otherwise supposedly insurmountable and painful situations. I discovered that most of the time I was basking in the dull light of my own prejudices and judgements about people whilst being gripped by the fear of failure or falling out of favour with the consensus.

Everyday life appeared to be easy if I followed the stereotypical thinking and remained in the communal cocoon. Living in the communal cocoon meant conforming with and meeting the terms of the society, no matter how unreasonable and compelling.

It is necessary for a true seeker of freedom to break from the enduring traditions if these traditions are unreasoned and compel obedience. An enlightened person is never enslaved by the unwritten, but rooted, laws that engender herd instinct and hinder expression of the inner-self. Such a person may at first be seen to be marching out of step with the rest of his companions but the truth is that he is listening and marching to the music of his own drummer. Such human beings epitomise individualism and courage of conviction

Rigidly following a tradition gives one an identity with a group and a solid attachment to it, but it separates one from all other groups and the higher spirit force. This is not to say that traditions and customs have no place in my life, or anyone's for that matter. Far from it; they are the vital pillars of any society.

There is a great deal to be said for living a

disciplined life that enables members of any community, be it social or economic, to interact as a cohesive, self-regulating group. It is a personal choice. Most people choose to conform rigidly because they see security in numbers. They prefer to be lost in numbers as one of a million rather than strive to be one in a million.

Gandhi said, *"Strength of numbers is the delight of the timid, the valiant in spirit glory in fighting alone"* – meaning those individuals who are lacking in strong self-belief, faith and self-motivation are insecure. They are devoid of spirituality and seek comfort from being part of a group. They conform and comply without questioning or reasoning. They are upright in the eyes of the society they live in, and that is what really matters to these individuals; whereas those who are truly gallant and ride on the back of natural principles are truly venturous. They are not driven by ego, but rather by a strong spiritual base that makes them self-driven, optimistic and fearless. They set their own very high standards and are not influenced by the opinions of the masses. They lead, rather than be led. They are prepared to question and challenge, and do not flinch in the face of adversity.

They are enlightened.

Enlightened individuals are the ones who

demonstrate the courage of conviction and follow the lone path to the divine eternity, and ultimately command respect of the fraternity. They do not bask in the dull light of ego that ordinary individuals do. They perceive and experience life in the wider spectrum of the divine light. To them seemingly insurmountable daily life circumstances are miniscule. They have the knack to experience rare insights and glimpses into the future. When Gandhi, in possession of a valid first class ticket, was thrown out of the train in South Africa, it is said that, lying on the platform of the railway station, in an instant he saw the whole of the British Empire crumble.

My coming to England gave me the opportunity to break loose from the proverbial shackles put on me by a community steeped in traditions.

I was free to make my own decisions – and thereby, was also responsible for the consequences of my actions. In spite of still being a student, that is an articled clerk, I made the choice to read for my professional examinations or go to see a film - any film - as I was a minor no more. To feel responsible for my own life was a major stimulus to my system. I could stay out till late at night and in the weekends sleep till mid morning. I could not believe that at barely twenty years of age I could go into a bar and order any alcoholic beverage, of course within my limits of affordability. I could tip a waiter much older, and earning more, than myself and be thanked for it. Once you were an adult, age did not matter so much, although there was the need to respect all, the young and the old alike. There were polite gestures as an integral part of daily intercourse with people. It was very natural, although at first alien to me, to routinely say 'please' and 'sorry' and 'thank you'.

One summer evening I asked an English man in a Kensington street to point me in the direction of Earls Court, which he did, whereupon I thanked him. He smiled and said, *"Pleasure's all mine"*. I could not believe that a man more than twice my age could speak to me so politely, take the trouble to give me precise directions and then call it his pleasure. I said to myself, *'Truly great people don't need to display authority with harsh language or put-on superior manner. Their greatness lies in the warmth and politeness of their graceful manner. These are the true ambassadors of their society'*.

This relatively minor incident was a great eye opener for me. I thought to myself if one man's behaviour can influence me to form an opinion about his people, it is natural that any impressions I make on any person who is not an Asian can lead to a generalised opinion about Indians. Because of this basic trait in most ordinary people I said to myself, I will cultivate good habits and mannerisms of an upright person and always endeavour to conduct myself in a way that will show Indians in a good light. I am their ambassador! At that stage of life I was still very much attached to the idea of classifying myself rigidly as an Indian.

I firmly started to believe that there were no restrictive forces to hold me back or self-appointed social architects to script my life. I was in charge. That also meant I could choose my friends - blacks, whites, Hindus, Moslems, Christians, Jews or any other; I could have any kind of hairstyle and wear any kind of clothing I liked. I felt I was a free man.

Like any undergraduate, I was self-deluded into believing that as soon as I qualified with a professional degree, life would be plain sailing as I would not have to suffer the drudgery of late nights with text books, sacrifice leisure activities like cricket and live under tension from lack of sufficient money. I would be able to command a respectable job and, with it, career prospects that would take me from strength to strength. I would have a status in my community and among friends. People would look up to me.

In reality it is not simple for one to command respect

of anyone until one feels respect deep down for one's own self, and when one actually learns to respect others. This has nothing to do with any kind of professional qualification. To sincerely respect another person is not easy, especially if one is imbued with stereotypically cynical views of other cultures, races, professions and social groups and is driven by all the accompanying prejudices.

Whilst I may not agree with certain cultural practices, habits, behaviours and anything else that is typical of a racial or any other group, I have no right to categorically resent it or condemn it, nor should I allow myself to stoop so low as to form generalised negative opinions about single individuals on the basis of their ethnic or racial background, or worse still about ethnic groups on the basis of the knowledge of single individuals. Needless to say that collectively human beings are a magnificent tapestry of rich colours and characteristics weaved by Nature.

I found that as I practised taking to bits the culture of narrow-mindedness and prejudice in me, I started to give myself access to a whole new and wonderful world that would have been denied me by my own ignorance. If I did not want anyone to judge me simply by reference to my ancestral label, I likewise had to re-programme myself never to form any rigid views about any individual without personally having true knowledge of that person. Reprogramming myself meant that in the inner I was signing a pact with Nature that I would endeavour, as best as possible, to live a life without prejudice against all races and religious groups. In return Nature had begun to work with me and, in the subconscious, guide me to remain as free as possible of any pre-judgments.

The real test for me came many years later in the aftermath of the 'Nine-Eleven' destruction of the World Trade Centre by anti-American Islamic terrorists. It is well-documented and appreciated that this event has had a serious transformational effect on not just the western hemisphere but the whole world.

In the immediate aftermath of the event came the strongest ever anti-Islamic fervour resulting in declarations being made by the American and certain other nations' leaderships to "fight terrorism". Most of the western world was moved by the event and began to be carried away by the call to fight terrorism. Every individual's life has been affected by the 'Nine-Eleven' event in its aftermath. I could sense anger and cynicism towards Moslems on the part of many people, including some of my friends and relatives. I found this initially to be spiritually most unsettling as I wanted no part in any hateful outpourings against any racial or religious groups.

There was turmoil in my mind. *"If the whole world is affected by this and is endeavouring to fight terrorism, what is my part in it? What do I have to do to make my contribution? I have no weapons or desire to physically fight or destroy anyone, including any terrorists. These terrorists chose to die, and more are willing to destroy themselves as suicide bombers, thinking that their cause will survive them, and those who die fighting for a cause, become martyrs. There are countless others who are waiting to die. These terrorist instincts, if indeed that is what they are, reside in the hearts of men and women who are passionate believers in a system. This is an ideological conflict, not a territorial war. These terrorists appear to be fighting for not any landmass or supremacy over other races and nations, but for respect, justice and fairness. They may appear to be hardened, unreasonable, intransigent, highly emotionally-charged, hateful and cynical. For harbouring these emotions they cannot be destroyed, but their emotions can be changed. This war is not won with weaponry, armaments, bombs and armies of soldiers. How can anyone engage in combat with someone who is willing to die anyway? That approach is futile. That being the case, how can anyone defeat such a person?"* I spent weeks in deep reflective contemplation and deliberated over this matter.

When I finally gave up striving hard for an answer, the Higher Force of inner wisdom came to my rescue. The answer came in a flash and stood right before my eyes. The idea should never be to defeat or deter such men and women, but rather to win a war jointly with them. This would be a war against intolerance, prejudice, cynicism, hatred, misunderstanding and the will to impose oneself on others, which are all common traits of basic ignorance in people of all races. This action would be all about truly reaching out and respecting – it would be a declaration of peace on war. I said to myself, *"In this crusade I can make a contribution, a significant contribution that would cost nothing and achieve a great deal."* Mother Theresa refused to take part in a march against the war in Vietnam, and said *"but do call me when you march for peace"*. How can this campaign be seen as a war against an enemy who cannot be seen, cannot be taken to any court of justice and exists in all of us?

I consciously began to change the way I viewed the followers of Islam. On the inside I began to truly show more goodwill, respect and love than I had done previously. I began to practise casting aside all remnants of petty prejudices against different ethnic groups. The holy Koran found a place on the bookshelf in my study and now I even occasionally observe the ritual of fasting during the month of Ramadan in my attempt to know what it is like to be a Moslem. Every time I met a Moslem I made a special effort to discuss Islam and the Moslem way of life and beliefs.

A true follower of Islam, by a very simple definition, is a humble, kind-hearted, respectful, charitable and loving human being, and so anyone who befits this description is a Moslem. It is so simple to define a Moslem but so difficult to inculcate in ourselves those qualities. By this definition I have been trying to become a Moslem all my life.

Consequently I have made some terrific friends and my life has become richer beyond imagination. I have a clear affirmation that generating goodwill, which comes from steadfast abstention from thoughts of harm toward others, is the only modus operandi for winning the war against terrorism. To abstain from an act of harm is only a half-measure, to cleanse oneself of even a thought of harm goes much further, but to proactively reach out to the perceived threat and seek reconciliation is simply divine.

This knowing has added a whole new dimension to my spiritual and psychological culture and given me a strong sense of security and massive inner strength. If I could personally benefit so much from adopting this approach, one can imagine what strides the human race can make towards peaceful co-existence by collectively doing so. It requires a firm and clear collective determination towards this end with constant and attendant thoughts which are gentle, but highly concentrated.

This belief of mine has been corroborated by the words of Dr. Martin Luther King, JR., *"The non-violent approach does not immediately change the heart of the oppressor. It first does something to the hearts and souls of those committed to it. It gives them a new self-respect; it calls up resources of strength and courage that they did not know they had. Finally it reaches the opponent and so stirs his conscience that reconciliation becomes a reality."* I came across these inspired words several months after I had begun to practise my belief, and reading them for me is an uplifting experience.

If groups of individuals committed to a common peace-seeking approach were to dedicate themselves to such an approach to achieving harmony, they would be able to reach and bring about positive influence remotely upon the hearts and conscience of their target subjects. This is borne out by words from Gandhi. He said, *"....the world of tomorrow will be, must be, a society based on non-violence. It may seem a distant goal, an unpractical utopia. But it is not in the least unobtainable, since it can be worked from here and now. An individual can adopt a way of life of the future without having to wait for others to do so. And if an individual can do it, cannot whole groups of individuals? Whole nations?"*

I am prepared to concede though that those who have contrary views on overcoming terrorism may have their justification for going to war on terrorism with massed weapons and armies of men. I acknowledge that this self-expression on the part of many millions of people in the world cannot be denied or curbed. The judgment as to which is the right approach will never be known for there is no finite time span by when the ultimate answer will be known. Each approach may be right in its own time. The decision to brand as terrorist and send to jail Nelson Mandela may have been justified as correct at that time by the South African regime but I challenge any person to come forward nearly five decades later and justify calling him a terrorist. Time outwits all, and it always wins and heals. The only prerequisite is to have patience, faith, hope and tolerance. These are matters of heart.

Mahatma Gandhi fought the British Empire on the principle of non-violence. Non-violence was not his only strength, but also respect for the British sense of justice and their judicial system and the principle that every nation has a right to self-determination. This belief coupled with a deep and genuine respect for his adversaries embedded in his consciousness won the day for him. He was guided by the principle that no people had a right to rule over other people without their consent, and for civilised people to surrender to the rule of other people was loss of self-respect.

In his non-violent, non-cooperation campaign for the independence of India, he was prepared to go to jail rather than lose self-respect by succumbing to an unjust rule. Non-violence was a tool, a weapon or a modus operandi employed by Gandhi, but the fight for his cause was founded on the knowledge that the British administration was just, sensitive and enlightened enough to see the need to respect the wish of the Indian people to become self-governing. He had dedicated himself to knowing and respecting the British, almost to the extent of becoming like one of them. Gandhi's positive influence reached the heart, soul and conscience of a large number of the British people.

Need for respect is universal. It is not a prerogative of a few. Everyone needs it. Loss of respect can drive a man to any lengths.

An episode in the life of Dedan Kimathi is a wonderful example of this. This was narrated to me by a Zambian friend of mine. Whilst the facts relative to this episode may not be entirely accurate, this narration nevertheless serves the purpose of conveying the essential message that the need for respect is universal, and a human being will go to extreme lengths to regain lost respect. I find it to be a touching story and often, when narrating it to friends, and particularly their children seeking guidance, I have felt a little tug in my heart.

Kimathi came to be recognised as a Kenyan national hero after the independence of his country. However, before independence, he was captured, branded a terrorist and executed in 1956.

A newspaper journalist once asked what it was that turned him into such a fierce fighter from being a harmless farmhand working for a white landowner in Kenya.

Dedan stated to this effect, *"Yes, that's true I was a farmhand working for a white bwana, and I was a loyal and very able man on the farm. He relied on me to carry out great many chores on the farm. He was a very kind and generous man. He looked after all the farm workers and we lived like a happy family. There was food, shelter, clothing, a clinic, a school for young children and lots of other livelihoods. Often I used to take workers' children for a ride on the back of the farm tractor which I was privileged to drive for short excursions. I was very popular and the children loved me. One day however, I must have been a little careless; I damaged a piece of very important equipment. This resulted in the power supply being cut off. The bwana got very angry and came striding towards me in a fury. Before I could say sorry, he slapped me across the face and refused to listen to my explanation. It was a rare mistake on my part, and the bwana's anger may have been justified. I stood there feeling helpless and ashamed. But there was a very serious lack of judgment on his part. When he hit me in the face, he overlooked the fact that my little boy, then only reaching my waist, was standing beside me. I was grossly humiliated.*

That evening when I went home, my son and my wife did not look me straight in the eye. They were both quiet and clearly most distraught. That night as I lay awake in bed, I realised how badly I had let down my son. I was no longer a hero in his eyes. I was no longer a man who could fix anything on the farm. I was a fallen man. I had lost his respect. Reflecting on this incident that night I decided that I would join the movement for the independence of Kenya, and to remove the foreign masters from my country so that no man ever has to suffer such indignity, and no little boy would have to lose the hero in his father – that no father is made to appear to his son as a feeble, helpless servant of a foreign master."

This is truly an amazing account of the length to which someone who thinks he is a fallen man can go to regain self-respect. To respect oneself means to have a deep sense of personal dignity, to allow self to come to the fore, to let one's own light shine, to be fearless in the face of all challenges, to value one's opinions and feel worthy of oneself. Every self-respecting person has feelings, emotions and desire to be liked and appreciated. To respect oneself, or another human being, even one's adversary, is most of all self-empowering. It is in self-empowerment that a person truly begins to feel liberated. That is because a self-empowered individual does not depend on others to make him feel good about himself. He or she is driven by a clear and meaningful purpose and the strength to fulfil it is derived from deep within.

SIX

EARLY EXPERIENCES

There is a lot to be learnt from the past, although I hasten to reiterate that past does not equal to the future, and I have no desire to use the past to justify or explain the present. It has been said we are all constantly changing, evolving and growing – some of us allow ourselves to be totally at the mercy of our social environment, whilst others endeavour to take charge of what happens to them – but in all cases we are in a constant state of change, coming from all kinds of influences. Everything we see and hear, and understand and digest is woven into the fabric of our consciousness and character. We are all products of our conditioning. As we think and as we receive and process information, so are we.

In my early years I, like any child, was totally at the mercy of the environment I lived in. What happened to me or around me affected the way I perceived life. From the time I was old enough to think about life and death, something inside me told me what I see and experience is not real – this is all a dream, I am something else and I have to find out what I am, or rather the real truth about me – for all around me there was abundant poverty, iniquity, injustice, disease, cruelty and indifference; so much so that it overwhelmed the love and joy there was also in life. It was not possible for life, as I saw it then, if it was real, to be so seemingly unfair. But my mother loved me and created a sense of the presence of a fair-minded and loving force somewhere that is responsible for creating the universe and which always cares and restores justice.

The origin of my belief in the existence of God lies in one childhood experience. I was about seven years old then. We used to live on a huge coffee and sugarcane estate near Kampala in Uganda. My father, who was a manager on the estate, enrolled my sister and me in a school in Entebbe, some twenty miles away. We used to go to school every morning in the back of a farm lorry and return in the evening. I found school in those days rather tiring and unexciting. Even at that age we used to be given homework. My teacher was not a nice person. She would punish pupils at the slightest of slip-ups. I found her to be unkind and frankly did not like her.

One morning I got up to find that I had not done my

homework. Admitting this to my mother or father was out of the question as it would have triggered more work as a punishment. So I manufactured a stomach-ache. This resulted in me being told to take a large spoonful of a liquid medicine that, I knew from past experience, was revolting to say the least. I was spared the agony of taking the medicine when I said I was all right. Shortly after we had bathed and had breakfast, it was time to leave for school. In the most despondent mood, head drooping, I climbed up into the back of the lorry and slumped against the near side, my lower back resting against it, knees bent and pointing upward, my face buried between them and my arms around my head as if I did not wish to be seen by the world.

I did not want the lorry to take me to school. I was too young to influence the driver in any way to extricate me from my predicament. The only course of action available was a plea to God! Yes, God!

I started to say silently and repeatedly, *"Oh God! Please stop this lorry"* or something to that effect. As best as I can recall, I was momentarily absent from my surrounding - I was away from myself. I do not know where I was or what was happening. I was in some kind of a vacuum. I cannot recall for how long I may have been in that state, but somehow, when I regained the sense of the present moment, I knew the lorry was going to stop.

Lo and behold! It broke down! This had never happened previously and there was no one in sight who could come to rescue us. It was long time before help arrived, and by then it was too late to go to school. I was filled with amazement and joy with a sense of gratitude. I had found a secret ally.

As I reflect back on this episode I can only say that this was a pure unadulterated mind at work. There was no doubt in my mind about the power of prayer. Whether one agrees with this, or not, is not the point, but the fact that I had a knowing that the truck was going to stop is.

A question arises here. Why did my belief in God not become stronger as I grew into a teenager? The answer is my expanding ego. Ego, through the mind, creates a delusional sense of an entity of importance of a physical palpable form called 'self' that has concern for the state of the physical body, looks, superiority over others, status and all such purposeless pursuits. It suppresses the formless entity and thus one's sensory talents for experiencing the invisible realities that exist in and around one. No wonder someone has called ego an acronym for 'Edging God Out'. During my plea for the truck to stop I had ended up completely surrendering myself to the Higher Force and found that momentarily I was fully merged with my surroundings. I was not an individual entity during those few moments.

I guess this is how I would have been when I was a newly-born child. I would have had no sense of self as an individual entity. Time and space would have been of no consequence to me. I would have been in a state of complete integrity, one with my surrounding, and under the protection of the divine force. I, like any other child, would have been without ego. Ego gives one a strong sense of individual presence in a material world that forms the context in which one measures one's own growth and success in life. As I was growing up I was constantly compared with other children at home and at school. It soon became apparent to me that life was all about success, and success was when I achieved something more than others did, or something unique. Life was all about competing and being noticed by all.

My father, and all of us, had now moved to Mbale, a small commercial town with a growing population. I was made aware that there were limited places in schools of higher education. After eight years of primary school education, on passing the final year examinations, one would progress to four years of secondary school education before going to university. Places in the main secondary school were limited. It was therefore critical to be in amongst at least the top half of the batch of students that sat for final year examinations set by the Ministry of Education. If you did not qualify for secondary education, you were branded as no good and brought a lot of grief to your parents.

Up to fourth grade at school I was a below average pupil. I could sense this from the way certain pupils were acknowledged and approved of by the teachers and by other pupils. I rarely participated in any discussions or group activities simply because I did not think I was up to that standard. I was always afraid of being mocked. I felt inferior. Any marks I scored in examinations did not attract any congratulatory feedback from anyone. I was nothing by my own measure and in the eyes of all around me. There was nothing noticeable about me.

However, I am certain that I had a very strong sense of ego or self-importance. I recollect an episode for which I am eternally ashamed and now can only sincerely beg forgiveness of this classmate victim of mine – a certain girl called Ida. This was when I was in grade three; some boys came to me and said that Ida was spreading rumours about me that I had a crush on a certain girl in the class. I was furious partly because it was a lie and partly because the subject girl wasn't exactly anyone special. My pride was hurt. My reputation was at stake!

Moreover, befriending anyone of the opposite gender at school or even gaining such reputation was a sure recipe for becoming a laughing stock.

The following morning, soon after assembly, on my way to the classroom, I tracked down Ida. She was standing on the steps just in front of a block of classrooms. I marched straight up to her as if in a fury and lifting my right hand, gave her a slap across the face.

She went into a state of shock and momentarily gazed at me with a quizzical expression on the face that was asking the question *"why?"* Then her complexion changed, her lips quivered and her eyes filled up with tears. She looked frightened. Before she could utter a sound I walked away without saying a word. I reported my action to my friends and this gave me a kind of relief that I had taken a step to safeguard my reputation. My friends were fascinated and looked at me with admiration for doing such a brave thing. I felt elated.

I was a seeker of such cheap popularity to make up for my mediocre performance in the classroom. In reality I was not at all happy in the classroom.

There was more sadness yet to come to my life. One Saturday evening I had gone to see a movie with a few of my friends. Half way through the film, someone came from behind and tapped on my shoulder. I turned back to see the face of an elderly friend of our family. He whispered to me in a rather sombre tone that I was wanted at home. I immediately sensed that something was wrong. When I reached home I heard my mother sobbing whilst seated on the edge of the bed next to my father who was lying there. He had died. This was after suffering a severe heart attack. He had had two such attacks prior to this. He had been a severe diabetic and fought it for several years but finally the dreaded disease defeated him. He departed at the age of only forty-three, leaving behind my mother and six children.

At that time I was too young to appreciate the severity of the effect of my father's death on my mother and the family. We moved into a smaller house, my elder brother having given up schooling and taken up full-time employment. My mother applied her sewing skills to making cotton-filled quilts at home to augment earnings brought home by my brother. In the same vein my elder sister took up tutoring small children outside her schooling hours. My mother dispensed with the luxury of having a domestic servant and took up responsibility for most of the domestic chores. She espoused thrift and frugality and practised it dutifully in running the household but without depriving us of basic necessities like good nutrition and appropriate clothing.

She practised thrift to the extent that the soapy water that remained after washing our clothes would be used in washing utensils after cooking, and yet five of us went to school wearing clothes which were washed and ironed everyday.

I found out that after my father's death, at the start of each new school term, unlike most other pupils, we were not required to pay fees. Our fees were paid from a special community fund set up for children from families with meagre resources. In the beginning I felt embarrassed, being seen and treated by other pupils as underprivileged.

Returning to my time at school, at the end of the fifth year, for some unexplainable reason, the school changed the way the examination results were announced. Instead of being given marks we were given grades, and guess what… I got an 'A'! I was so elated that I rode on a friend's bicycle down the road and made it known to all the residents of the entire neighbourhood that I had scored an 'A'. Then on the first day at school in the new-year, during a frank and lively discussion about the previous year's results with the class master, all the 'A' graders were rather keen to find out who actually came first. The teacher was not forthcoming and, when I beseeched him to tell us, his rather sharp response was *"Don't worry, it wasn't you!"*

There was laughter all round and I felt, not only very humiliated, but insulted. The inference was that no-one in the class expected me to be the one. I was a mediocre pupil. Ida was there and she knew it too. That was the first time in my life then that I really felt hurt. I sensed I had become a bit of a laughing stock amongst the elitist, bright pupils in my class. My pride was truly hurt.

This was followed by another incident with my science master that I now regard as life transformational. One afternoon during class I was rather heroically more disruptive than usual. The teacher, Mr. M, stopped all proceedings and walked up to me. Then, in a quiet but stern voice, commanded me to follow him. There was total silence in the classroom as everyone was stunned and sat wondering as to what was happening. This kind of measure was unprecedented. I was escorted to the science laboratory. He closed the door and asked me to stand in the middle of the floor. I stood in silence and watched apprehensively whilst he pulled all the black cotton curtains. Suddenly the laboratory was totally dark.

He took hold of the wooden blackboard pointer from a cupboard and stood in front of the room and gazed at me for a few seconds. It seemed like an eternity. I feared I was going to be a recipient of some serious corporal punishment, and thought to myself that I did not deserve such humiliating treatment, which was only meant for some of the really notoriously mischievous older boys who were renowned for regularly taking such punishment. They were the scourge of the school and no-one respected them. I did not deserve to be branded as one of them.

Most fortunately Mr. M chose to refrain from what I was fearing the most, and instead preferred to address me verbally. I listened to him. It seemed he spoke from his heart and was at pains to deliver his message. He spoke for a few minutes and I listened to him intently, still fearing he would strike me afterwards. He put the pointer away and continued to speak. I was somewhat relieved and began to digest what was being said. The essence of his message was that I was not only failing to pay attention to what was being taught in the classroom, but worse still I was preventing other pupils from learning. He reminded me that it was essential for me to gain good education as I was of a poor economic standing. My fees were being paid by some of those pupils' parents who made contributions to the community fund, and therefore I was being ungrateful and should be ashamed of myself. Their investment in me was being wasted, and I was being ungrateful by disrupting their children's education.

I was visibly shaken up by what he said and broke down as I acknowledged my shameful behaviour. Momentarily I wished the ground would open up from under my feet and take me in. It seemed life was not worth living. He waited patiently whilst I recomposed myself and then we returned to the classroom. Some of the pupils were inquisitive, whilst others speculated and chuckled amongst themselves.

I was quite sad for a few days and remained generally quiet. A deep feeling of shame had taken a hold on me. I genuinely felt sorry for my behaviour and made a firm resolution that I would not allow myself to be ridiculed in the classroom again. This brought about a certain kind of metamorphosis in me. My general demeanour changed and I began to take life at school more seriously. And this marked a new beginning for me.

Consequently, that year I got down to some serious work and made real effort to take in what was taught in the classroom. I paid concerted attention to what was being taught, and followed it up with extra effort towards revision at home every afternoon. My mid-term and half-year results were encouraging. The hard work was showing good results, and this motivated me to excel in the end-of-year examinations; and I did! The reward for it all was my being called up at the open day event to receive a set of three Enid Blyton books for coming first in my entire batch of sixth year pupils. This was in presence of the entire school and many parents. I felt elated, but managed to contain my exhilaration.

My reputation was enhanced and other pupils began to talk about me in wonder. I am sure some of those parents also felt that their investment in my education was paying a dividend in the sense that I was setting a good example for their children.

At home I began to be seen as a grown up and an intelligent person. The Blyton books found a place on the shelf at home amongst our collection of Hindu classics. The thing about this success and the praise showered on me by family and friends was that now I had to live up to everyone's expectations for the future. They saw me as a very intelligent adolescent, and I also became aware that some parents chided their children for failing to *become like Anil"*. A high standard was set for me. Fortunately I was able to take up the challenge and never experienced failure at school, or in my professional examinations thereafter. Without meaning to sound smug, I do say that I was a regular prize winner!

But the most uplifting thing I experienced then was

a remark made by the headmaster, Mr Kailash, who was feared by all pupils and some of the junior teachers too. Being tall, broad shouldered and carrying military-style deportment, he was authoritative and had a presence about him. He spoke with a strong domineering voice that would not only fill the entire room but also unwittingly de-genius most of us. He used to thrive in taking impromptu classes, I guess, to test the standard of teaching in his school. During one such English revision session in the final term of the eighth year, preparatory to the critical secondary school entry examinations, he appeared in my class, unannounced, in place of our regular English teacher. He said he was taking the class on that day, and we froze as he began with a torrent of random questions fired at us. There was no doubt that some of us, who failed to deliver prompt answers, were having a torrid time. After about a long half hour of agonising questions, met by unsatisfactory responses from most of the class, he got quite animated, and dealt his final blow as expressed his disappointment at the lack of preparedness on our part. Pointing a finger at me, he said, in a rather prescient tone, to the rest of the class, *"He has all the answers and appears to be the only one who is prepared. I don't hold much hope for the rest of you,"* and made an exit to everyone's relief. Inwardly I was delighted but chose to contain myself as the real test of my endeavours was yet to come.

The eighth year at school brought another success, of a different kind, on the sports field. I was not just a book nerd. I used to play street cricket and was a rather keen player. My interest came, at the age of seven, from accompanying my father to the Sunday match at the Indian Sports Club in Kampala. I used to sit all day and watch the bowlers and batsmen in action whilst my father played cards. Cricket held a kind of appeal for me. I was particularly taken by all the gear worn by the players, the white flannels and shirts, metal-studded shoes, multi-coloured peaked caps, white leg guards and leather gloves. There was more etiquette, ritual and ceremony to the game when English cricketers were present. They liked to play in the grandest of cricketing razzmatazz, befitting a typical colonial setting. There was always a splendid spread of cakes, pies and snacks at teatime. On odd occasion some kind player offered me a plateful of these delicacies which I gratefully received and took no time to polish off.

For the first time in the history of the school inter-house cricket was introduced, to be played on a league basis. And guess what? Yours truly, who belonged to Blue House, was asked to open the batting for the House and scored 55 runs in a match-winning effort. My House won the league that year and my maiden inning's score remained a record in the primary school for a few years as far as I can recall. Younger pupils started to look up to me. Several girls in the school began to admire me. I hoped Ida was one of them as I really wanted her to forgive me. Some of them became my sister's friends; I guess to get close to me.

There was another intervening incident though which I recall quite vividly. In one of the ensuing matches another boy from Blue House scored 52 runs and remained not out. I overheard a rather heated debate one day amongst some enthusiastic boys that his score was better than mine as he had remained not out on 52. That there was a contrary view amongst some schoolboys was not acceptable to me. My reputation was being dented. I was compelled to immediately start a lobby group to defend my position on the grounds that '*nonetheless my score was greater, and that is what counts in the final analysis*'.

It is evident that I had become very aware of myself and the opinions of others were beginning to matter quite a lot. How I performed in the class, on the cricket field and in other extra-curricular activities like elocution, drama and debates mattered. My looks mattered. Whatever others had to say about me mattered. And as long as all of this went well and was positive, I felt good about myself. I was approved. Any adverse comment about me, or my failure to live up to a standard I set for myself, was demoralising. Fortunately there were only a few occasions when I felt demoralised. I was engrossed in myself. My ego had taken a stranglehold on me!

The big 'I' was beginning to matter. I was now an individual entity and my every achievement, every success was, I began to believe, due to my own efforts. Whilst I had been taught at home by my mother that all inspiration to perform great feats comes from the universal force, and for this one should remain constantly grateful to the Almighty, I paid only scant regard to this. I did not truly understand, nor did I take the trouble to understand, the meaning of being an instrument of the Almighty. Compiling content for self appeared to be more gratifying than connecting with the essence of the self. I had a personal life agenda to take care of – that is I had various different roles to play in life – I had to become someone who would be recognised by others as a role model, a specialist in a field of knowledge, a holder of titles, an athlete or a performer of some kind, a lover, a husband, a father, an industrialist, a tycoon, a leader or anyone else that others would look up to and see as successful. Thus carving out of life a fitting definition for me had become paramount.

The process of my social and psychological conditioning had now taken a firm hold on me. I was well and truly in the pickle jar. I was beginning to see myself in my imagination. My image of myself would dictate my future behaviour. My self-image was positive, but was it real?

SEVEN

DISILLUSIONMENT

When I qualified as a chartered accountant in 1973, I applied to and succeeded in upgrading myself by joining a reputable City firm of accountants in the part of London commonly known as the Square Mile. The firm then was boasting a place amongst pantheons of accounting practices - the top five in the country - and was a leading name in the world.

The greatest immediate benefit to someone freshly minted like me was that there was a quantum leap in salary which in my case went up from a princely sum of fifteen pounds a week to forty two pounds a week, and even more when my salary was increased by a staggering fifty percent after one year in the firm. To put the value of the money into perspective let me say that fifteen pounds a week before tax was sufficient for a single individual to live on comfortably in London after paying for accommodation and transport.

This was a matter of great pride for my family as I was able to apply for a mortgage and succeeded in acquiring a four-bedroom house in Luton, an industrial town renowned for being a home to Vauxhall motors and an airport. I was then an audit senior - only a junior rank amongst all the professionals in the firm. Audit and taxation were my specialities. I would like to say that I became quite popular amongst those clients of the firm I was detailed to audit. To put my new annual salary into perspective I recall that the cost of my first house was just under four times my salary.

Initially I had found the going in this new employment a little tough, felt introverted and out of place. There was no-one to hold my hand and show me all the ropes. I had to find out the administrative practices of the firm the hard way. I was in due course able to find my way round and distinguish partners from staff, and managers from others. Soon I settled down and started to feel comfortable. As I accomplished my assignments, I was able to get to know my departmental manager a little better and met relevant partners during audit reviews. I gained an impression that they were generally pleased with the quality of work I turned out, and this was evidenced in the healthy pay increase I was awarded after one year of service.

Here I found myself to be amongst fellow professionals and trainees who were, in terms of sophistication, a notch or two above those old colleagues of mine with whom I qualified in Hammersmith, a suburb of West London. Most of my new colleagues were graduates from recognised universities seeking accountancy qualification as a stepping-stone to eventual high positions in commerce and industry. Some were sons of highly placed fathers in reputable companies and public offices. They were all fiercely competitive and ambitious. Each one was an individual entity, essentially looking after the interest of "number one". Preoccupied with self, none had time or inclination to make friends with colleagues. A kindred spirit was hard to find. This culture was alien to me, but I had to experience it.

This was all during major catastrophic happenings in the British industry. The economy was out of control with soaring unemployment, double digit inflation and mounting balance of payments deficit. Rolls Royce, the pride of the British industry had gone into liquidation and was being revived through reconstruction. The coal miners' winter strike had resulted in the nation working a three-day week to conserve energy. The Government had set up the Prices and Incomes Board to regulate price and wage increases, and the accountancy profession was hotly debating inflation accounting to portray realistic financial states of affairs of major companies. A fiscal measure known as stock relief had been introduced to avoid taxing inflation profits.

All these happenings posed a minefield for the unwary accountant. During these times possession of the latest information and knowledge, not freely shared with other audit seniors, was an invaluable facilitator of one-upmanship. No-one cherished the idea of voluntarily sharing information with colleagues on the latest developments in accounting standards and disclosure rules, or in commerce and industry, or in the Ministry of Finance, all of which impacted on the individual professionalism and thus on the well-being of the firm.

This was all a major culture shock to my system, but I convinced myself that it was a character builder. *"It will see me in good stead one day"* I kept repeating to myself. In my old firm, where I was an articled clerk and where I qualified, most of the trainees were taught by senior and qualified colleagues. It was part of the firm's culture to share knowledge and support everyone's professional progress. We celebrated one another's success, no matter how small, in dealing with clients' affairs and in professional examinations. This was one big family in which all the partners were easily accessible to staff, and were aware of every individual's progress in the firm.

There were very few women professionals in my new firm, and those that I knew were highly charged with a burning desire to succeed. It must have been extremely difficult in those days for women to make strides in this male-dominated profession. I had nothing but admiration for those few female colleagues I shared assignments with and was at first rather fascinated to see them engage in discussions on all kinds of subjects with their male colleagues as their social equals. Those that progressed to more senior positions even supervised teams of male members of staff. Whereas this may have been quite normal for everyone, it was not so for me, having been raised in an environment where a woman's place was firmly in a home, or in workplace in a support role of some kind.

My first experience that quashed this stereotype to some extent was during my second year of articleship, with my old firm, after I had successfully passed my intermediate examination, and was therefore deemed fit enough to handle certain audit assignments as a supervisor. One of my colleagues, PG, who had not been so fortunate with his accountancy examinations, had previously been in charge of this specialist floral products firm's audit. He was instructed to handover the client's file to me. During the initial briefing from the partner in-charge I gathered that the client was a woman, which to me meant that this assignment would not be much of a challenge. I assumed I was being patronisingly initiated into seniority with this small file. It was good customary practice for any new audit assignee to be introduced to the client by the previous incumbent, and so PG took me to meet the client and explained the entire audit procedure to me. I was introduced to Mrs. B. She was a rather stocky and overbearing woman who had a presence about her, not unlike my primary school headmaster. She welcomed me with a condescending smile and perfunctory handshake whilst fully absorbed in expressing her pleasure to PG at seeing him again after several months. They chatted for a while about business in general, local politics and the economy. Then PG introduced me to all the floral firm's staff and briefed me on how and where all the records were kept. It was then time for him to return to the office, leaving me behind to progress with the audit. But to my horror Mrs. B took umbrage that the assignment was being relegated to me. She refused to let PG return to the office and said indignantly that I was *too young to be left alone to do the work, I needed to be supervised.* After much persuasion, and only when told that I was more qualified to conduct the audit than PG, she relented, but frankly did not appear to be convinced.

I was unsettled by her overt display of disapproval

of me as the sole auditor of her books. This seeming doddle of an assignment now became a major hurdle to climb for a chartered accountant in the making. My ego was shattered even before I commenced my first audit. *'There is no doubt all in the office will have a laugh at my expense when they hear about it. This is a bad start'* I said to myself. The client did not value my presence and going back to the office to say she did not approve of me was like returning from a battlefield, shamefully defeated and wounded. I was well and truly caught between the dragon, a proverbial dragon I hasten to add, and the deep sea, but decided to soldier on in spite of the fact that for the first few days Mrs B chose to stay away from me. She left me to get on with my work.

I am certain she felt uneasy as she had to swallow her pride in the presence of half a dozen of her own staff and succumb to PG's insistence that I needed no supervision. There were matters I had to raise with her in the later course of the audit, and so I made a spirited effort to see her. At first she appeared to be disinclined to engage, with any warmth, in any discussions with me as in her eyes I was a mere clerk, but my persistence eventually led to her feeling a little more at ease. As she gradually warmed to me and began to part with information for me to complete my tasks, both of us felt quite relaxed about approaching the other.

Finally when discussing draft accounts with her I noted that she demonstrated a firm hold on her floral products business that was profitable and growing. My recommendations for improvements in controls impressed her so much that she became inquisitive about my background, family, reasons to become a chartered accountant and so on.

On the final day of the audit I was treated to a customary lunch when she apologised for her histrionics which she said was out of character, but brought on by the fear of the unknown. She thought I was very intelligent and admitted being impressed with the manner in which the audit had been so expeditiously conducted in record time. Amid all the praises showered on me, she did say that at first she found me to be a little arrogant. I think at the first sight of me she had sensed my chauvinistic attitude towards women. However, my ego was not only restored, but blown up severalfold when she enquired if I could spare the time on Saturdays to help her with bookkeeping and in return earn some extra income. Unfortunately I had to decline on the grounds that I was still studying to qualify, and so could not spare the time. She commended me to the partner for excellent service. I guess that was her way of apologising to him.

This experience was a great eye opener and I was determined that I was not going to fall foul of any female colleagues in the new firm where some of the more senior partners were knighted, quite a few held honorary public offices, some were personal advisors to famous personalities and heads of state, some belonged to various other professional bodies and held positions in the Institute of Chartered Accountants that enabled them to influence professional and ethical standards. I was amongst the elite of the professionals in the country. Their mannerisms gave clear impressions that they all regarded themselves as superior members of the human race.

We worked in stuffy offices with no fixed places to sit for most of the staff, except assistant managers and above. All audit staff were meant to be out on assignments earning fees, and the less they were in the office the more it was possible to charge time to clients. Parallels were drawn with airlines – if the aeroplanes were standing idle on the ground, they were not earning income. We were revenue centres charged out at four times our basic salary. It was paramount that we justified our existence by generating revenue for the firm.

As time went by and as I was charged with more demanding assignments, I began to realise that I was merely assisting the process of statutory compliance imposed by law under the Companies Act on the clients to have their accounts audited and certified. If there was no such requirement, I would be redundant.

All the clients of this firm were reputable companies, organisations and partnerships with ample resources to serve all the requirements of the business and meet the aspirations of their owners. The key employees of these organisations were rewarded for their contribution. There was very little value an auditor was able to add to the clients' internal controls and procedures, or to their growth and profitability.

I felt as if I was doing very little constructive work, if any, for the client in return for a fat fee for my employer. The extent of the audit work I carried out was substantiated by my audit file and the quality of my work was determined by the state of the file and the evidence therein of all the programmed test checks, vouching and enquiries made to satisfy my employer that all was well, and so an unqualified audit report could be issued.

Such was the weight of the audit report that in the event of it being qualified - meaning that the auditor was not fully satisfied that all the key systems and controls were proper, or there total transparency of all the material transactions which could be verified or the auditor could reach an opinion that the financial statements gave a true and fair view of the state of the affairs of the business as a going concern - serious repercussions would ensue such as directors having to make a declaration of non-compliance with lender's covenants, withdrawal of financing facilities by lenders, or a lowering of credit rating resulting in collapse of the market value of its shares quoted on the stock exchange, and so on.

In the event of any litigation or claim by the client that the auditor failed to diligently carry out proper checks, the only evidence in defence was contained in the audit file. This file had to stand the scrutiny of the court to absolve my employer of any oversight or carelessness. Eventually, it seemed, to my employer the state of the audit file was more critical than the quality of the actual audit work carried out.

In those days accountancy practices in the main were not exposed or susceptible to the competitive forces of the market. There was no real effective monitoring of the standards prevailing in these practices, or rather there was no need for formal regulation; simply because members of public institutions were meant to be ethical, honourable and fair-minded people with a strong sense of social responsibility.

The Institute of Chartered Accountants in England and Wales operates under a Royal Charter, working in the public interest. Chartered accountants were, and still are, meant to possess professional expertise and integrity having undergone the correct and intensive training, the same being true of doctors, teachers and lawyers.

Legally, anyone can carry the label 'accountant' without the necessary training and experience. But before becoming a 'Chartered Accountant' and applying the letters ACA or FCA after his or her name, an individual with a recognised college degree undergoes a period of at least three years of training as an articled clerk with a recognised firm of chartered accountants, and passes tough examinations covering accounting and book-keeping, financial management, auditing, commerce and business strategy, taxation and information technology before exercising the charter to certify the accounts of a legal body. And most importantly, the Institute members are expected to maintain high standards of ethical and professional conduct.

I was trained and qualified with those impressions of my profession.

Having been in this firm for just over two years, I began to ask myself, *'What am I doing here, why am I here and where is this taking me?'* I was working long hours and earning a good income, but truly speaking I was not happy. I had capitulated to the swagger of the professional city gents in pin-stripe suits, and had no courage to move from there because I was afraid of the possible ensuing castigation, shame and humiliation.

Frankly I did not know what to do and chose to stay put, hoping that something would somehow happen.

Nature was at work again. Choosing to stay put meant leaving things to the Higher Force. My decision was soon made for me following an incident in the office. One late afternoon, I had reason to go to my manager's office. He shared his office with the assistant manager. They were both in the office, and in deep discussion. I stood in the doorway concealed from them by the door that was half-open, and was about to knock on the door to request entry into the office when I overheard my manager say out loud enough for me to hear, *"Kumar will have to be twice as good as anyone here to go any further"*. This was the time of the year to consider promotions and salary reviews. I could not believe what I had just heard, and stood there unnoticed for a few seconds. Thereafter, I turned round and stealthily went back to my seat, absolutely stunned. I spent the rest of the afternoon ruminating, as my mind became alive with the memory of the experience with the college principal.

A few days later, promotions were announced and sure enough yours truly was overlooked. The message was loud and clear. One or two other junior and less experienced colleagues were promoted. I was not wanted as anything other than an audit senior. I had to go. My decision was made for me.

Within a few weeks I secured a position outside the profession in a manufacturing company in Hertfordshire as a Financial Accountant. I was quite prepared to suffer the humiliation of having to tell my friends and relations that I had resigned from the job, effectively implying failure to make a career in the City firm. I was not going to mention racial prejudice to anyone as a reason to leave. I did though have a plausible reason for the change in career in that my new employment included a brand new 1.6 litre Ford Escort.

I was extremely saddened by the episode at the City firm, but was happy to put this short stint down as an experience. I could not believe that even amongst such groups of highly educated professional individuals thinking and decision-making were tainted with, what I think, racist instincts. The man ceased to be a manager in my mind, lost my respect and sank very low in my esteem. In those days there were no real grievance rules in any firm, or any legislation against racial practices in workplace.

But even if legislation had existed, I would not have exercised my right to be protected by it. I do not believe what is in a person's heart can be changed by law. Law will stop a person uttering hateful words at someone of a different race or colour, but not eradicate hatred from the person's heart, it may stop a person from discharging me from employment without justification, but it will not enthuse such a person to hire me in the first place.

By resigning I lost nothing, but rather gained an entry into a whole new world away from an environment devoid of human warmth – I likened the firm to a busy railway station accommodating indifferent travellers for short periods on a common platform before they proceed on their individual paths – not conducive to proper nurturance of my inner-self. For me staying there any longer would have been like waiting for a bus in a street where buses did not run.

To this day I am convinced that this was not a cowardly action on my part. What resides in a person's mind and heart, one cannot eliminate with rhetoric or enforcement of one's rights. There was no need for any melodramatic fight to be treated equally. This was just one person in a firm run otherwise by honourable and fair-minded members of the profession I was a part of. I like to think he has since learnt a lot about life and people.

I bore no grudge, nor ill will towards him. Indeed, if anything, there was a case to express gratitude for him being instrumental in bringing a realisation in me as to how detrimental and destructive racial prejudice can be to an innocent person's livelihood. In retrospect this was a constructive experience for me, an awakening. How I felt about this first-hand experience of racial prejudice made me go deep inside with a question as to why man's behaviour is so riddled with indifference and disregard for fellow human beings.

It brought back memories of the incident at the college and triggered the process of deep thought and reflection once again. Could it be that this episode was a reflection of my own inner thoughts and prejudices? Could it be that I had seen a part of me in him? Could it be that he had a part to play in my spiritual unfolding?

According to the ancient Vedic science the outer world we experience is the manifestation of the inner world we create for ourselves through prior conditioning and experiences. This was no mere coincidence. Coincidence can be construed ordinarily to indicate a random occurrence of an event without any causal connection. But I saw this event as a coincidence in a Vedic context, meaning a happening or coming together of two events with a definite purpose. I am of a firm belief that this event was destined to happen sooner or later. My own inner-self needed cleansing; this experience was the prompt.

We are all responsible for all that happens to us. He reflected instincts in me which bore hallmarks of deep-seated prejudices and judgmental attitude towards people of colour and other religious inclinations. I realised I was up to my neck in it. I had inadvertently become judgmental and cynical about great many of my colleagues in the firm, about their social behaviour, their society, habits and culture. And what about how I had viewed native Africans in Uganda prior to coming to England? I was only experiencing what I had consciously and sub-consciously meted out to Africans for so many years. And if I didn't do it directly, I certainly condoned the whole process of prejudice against Africans practised by Asians and Europeans. I had so much to put right about myself.

In the manufacturing company, the other side of the fence as it were, I began to realise that I could make a difference. No sooner had I settled down in this organisation that was manufacturing lampshades, wallpapers and various paper products, than I began to enjoy a sense of fulfilment from my profession. I was part of a small management team and active in the real decision-making process. The introduction of a computerised accounting system in this organisation remains as one of my most cherished achievements in life for the reason that for the first time in my life I had taken the courage and responsibility for doing something that made a positive difference to the way other people did their work and benefited the company.

It gave me a strong and lasting self-belief and realisation of my capabilities. I was responsible for my discipline and stood as an authority on accounting and finance in the whole company.

This was the beginning of a whole new experience and once again gave me the affirmation that whatever happens, no matter how disheartening at first, always happens for the best.

I put the experience in the City firm behind me, and

made a commitment to working where I was part of a creative process. But even here there was another lesson to be learnt. Living is experiencing. I had no predecessor in my new job, but there was a gentleman, a part-qualified accountant and much older than myself, who used to perform some of the accounting work in the firm before I arrived. Upon my arrival most of his accounting responsibilities and several additional ones were placed on my shoulders.

Having made early impressions, I became popular with the directors and other employees of the company, except one person and it does not take a genius to figure out who this would be. Our relationship lacked warmth and generally we did not say to each other more than was necessary. It was essential for us to work as a team. Whilst he sat in the directors' monthly board meetings and was privy to a great deal of corporate information, he was often rather less than economic when it came to sharing essential information with me. This caused me embarrassment at times as I was made to look incompetent. It was extremely difficult to work with him.

Information is power. Young, ambitious and talented people, if fed with information and properly guided and nurtured, can become a powerhouse of creativity and productivity. They are quick learners and have high mental stamina and retentive memory. Not having experienced failure, they generally have no inhibitions, nor any fear of failing. They can pick themselves up quickly after a setback. Their burning desire to put matters right and succeed galvanises them into action rapidly. Lack of experience in youth is often made up for by their enthusiasm, stamina for hard work and hunger for success. This was me!

To hold back such individuals out of fear that they may put us to shame or make a serious mistake is an unforgivable frittering away of the wealth of a society.

This particular experience taught me to see young qualified individuals in a different light, certainly different to that in which I was seen by him. I have long found collaborating with young talent as a joyous experience. I see in young people opportunities to re-live my life and help them attain what I may not been able to achieve in my youth. A combination of piquant and zestful experience on the one hand and talent, stamina and zeal on the other is a perfect recipe for fabulous success. There is no fear or shame in acknowledging a young and more talented person.

Nevertheless, there was a limit to the extent to which I could endure the daily battles with this man who was bent on trying to maintain an upper hand on me. Any changes in procedures and systems I introduced for the better were scuppered by him. It hurt my pride that reforms I introduced were being undermined. He was not at all receptive to change.

Finally I decided to quit. I secured a position nearer to my home at a higher salary. But it was not that simple. When I submitted my letter of resignation to the managing director, he refused to accept it. Instead I was invited to a private dinner that evening. I explained nearness of the new employment to my home as my justification to leave. This was countered by his heart softening expression of regret that I was leaving for such a trivial reason without prior discussion with him. He considered me as a highly talented accountant with potential to go far in the company. For my immaturity and naïveté, I allowed myself to be influenced by his remarks. He made it clear that I was badly needed. I retracted my resignation. In return he raised my salary. My characteristic deference to seniors and fear of causing unpleasantness prevented me from disclosing the real reason.

I could not understand why, in spite of all his shortcomings, this gentleman was not being released from work or relieved of those duties which were clashing with my role in the company. I felt rather ashamed of myself for having succumbed to the MD's flattering words and an improved package. Otherwise there was no change in the situation at work. I did subsequently resign a few months later when the balance finally swung in favour of the need for job satisfaction. I could not be stopped this time as I was most determined to leave.

A few years later, after I had made a major career change, I called to see the MD socially. He was thrilled to see me and brought me up to date with all the wonderful things that were happening in his company. He wished I was still with him and actually hoped I would be tempted to return. This was truly great for my ego, but he was disappointed when I explained that I was really doing very well in my new overseas employment. At that juncture I plucked enough courage to tell him that I owed him my real reason for leaving. He was unmoved as if he had known about it all along and opened up to me to explain the situation regarding the individual, who was now semi-retired.

I was taken by his explanation and, although he was a chartered accountant like me, my previous preconceived notions about him went out of the window when I heard his philosophy on managing and interacting with people. I used to think he was a numbers man like me. That evening I came to realise that he was much more than an accountant.

He portrayed his real self as a wonderful compassionate human being who cared firstly for people and then for business profits. He spoke as a very good leader who deserved rightly to be the managing director of the company. He said to the effect that one often talks about an employee's loyalty to the company, but there is also the reverse of this. A good employer has to be loyal to his employees. During the infancy of the company, the subject individual made a significant contribution to its growth, and worked long tireless hours because the company could not afford to employ more people. He was always there and never looked at the clock to see the time of the day or the calendar to see the day of the week. He had a vast knowledge of the company's activities. Its major customers had immense respect for him. He was trusted by all senior people in the company and was always there when needed. No value could be placed on his devotion to the company. The company chose to accommodate him in spite of all his shortcomings.

He talked about the importance of placing people at the centre of every action of any corporation. The greatest attribute of successful leaders is that they do not see everything in the frame of rules and established practices, or as black and white, and simplify all of their decision making by firmly landing on one side or the other of a clear dividing line between right and wrong, but rather seek to manage the grey margin in the middle and the wider the margin the greater the challenge for them. It is in this margin, the corridor of the hidden truth, that true leaders seek success with people. It is here that their patience and perseverance are tested and developed. It is here, in the grey margin, where true leaders of men are made and become winners in the long run.

What a contrast between this accountant and the other one in the City firm!

One other small confusion he cleared for me was that those business leaders who possess the ruthless streak to relocate, hire and fire people at will, supposedly in the interest of business, are often concerned with self-preservation and image. They are accountable to owners who are less visible in business and generally tend to be institutions, trusts, corporate bodies and large groups of individuals. In direct contrast to them are owners, or families, working in and managing successful and highly reputed businesses, which always see their employees as partners and indispensable assets of the business. They remain eternally grateful to their employees for being instrumental in the success of the business. To them their employees are not pawns on a chess board available to be sacrificed for a misperceived greater good. He cited an example of a successful family-owned company whose shareholders upon reaching retirement age gave the ownership of the company to its employees who had loyally contributed to its growth.

There was one other faith-restoring experience I had prior to this one. At the time we bought our house in Luton, house prices had started to rise. Buyers would panic and push to complete the deals as soon as possible, and sellers would delay the process in the hope that someone would enter the fray and offer a higher price. This process, known as gazumping, was becoming quite common. A few weeks after I had paid a deposit on our house, the estate agent called me and said the owner of the property was withdrawing the house from the market. This was most disheartening as we had really worked hard to locate this particular large four-bedroom house which was just right for my wife and mother and sisters and brothers, and really we had all fallen in love with it. This was going to be the first tangible asset of our family. I protested to the agent, but only succeeded in finding out the name of the owner. The house belonged to a church. I wrote to the head of the management body that was responsible for the administrative and financial affairs of the church. In my letter I stated the circumstances of our family and made a plea for a special consideration, whilst also stating that I did not believe that a church would knowingly go back on its word for an additional commercial gain. Deep within I had a knowing that there would be a favourable response. I had been saying to myself, *The people who are responsible for the assets of this church live by the Christian principles of love, understanding and charity. The fact that we are a non-Christian immigrant family will not work against us, rather, if anything, it will assist. People come before profit."*

I received a reply by return to the effect that the property was back on offer to me and the lawyers would proceed with the completion. My respect for and faith in people connected with the running of ecclesiastical bodies was enhanced. It has not diminished to this day, decades later.

Dissatisfaction at work was not the only factor that spurred me to take up an overseas employment. Whilst I was with the manufacturing company, I became a proud father of my first son. My wife, a nurse and a midwife, gave up her job as a ward sister in a state hospital to raise him. It was her desire to stay away from employment until he was old enough to go to school.

This was the time in Britain in the mid-nineteen-seventies when the economy was still in turmoil. The effect of the first ever major international oil price increase in the early part of the decade was now beginning to tell. Unemployment had reached 1.4 million, the interest rate was running at more than 10% and inflation at above 15%. The unions were becoming more difficult to contend with, obviously for understandable reasons. There were rampant strikes in all the major industries and public services. Trains and buses were hit the hardest. Fares soared above average inflation. Within three months after I had become the sole breadwinner in my family, I had to draw money out of our savings account to meet monthly living expenses. We had become accustomed to saving a fraction of our monthly earnings, but now this virtuous practice was under threat. I was quite distressed by this deteriorating economic environment.

Secondly, the very house we had all fallen in love with became a lonely place for me. Within two years of us coming to the house, my sisters and brothers got married and went to their respective homes. My mother decided that she would rotate between all of us and went initially to live with my younger brother. All of a sudden from being part of a close-knit family of brothers and sisters living with mother, I was alone in the house with only my wife our one-year old son, Nick. It was very quiet in the house, especially during the evening meal times and weekends which reminded me of the times when we all used to have so much to talk about. My two younger sisters and brother were the budding stars who had so much to say about their achievements and embarrassing moments at work. My elder brother, who was mostly dedicated to our well-being, was still at the centre all decision making. All six of us were working and living under one roof with our mother. This enabled us to save up and prosper. Between us, in total contrast to our days in Uganda when the only means of transportation we had was my elder brother's bicycle, we were now proud owners of three motorcars.

Although neither of us ever said it, Umi and I knew we were not happy with life, detached from the rest of the family. We did not really like living in this large house any more. It was no longer a home. We were not happy. We needed a change. The need was intense and something had to happen.

One Sunday afternoon I saw an advertisement in the weekend paper and said to her, *"Fancy going back to Africa?"* She promptly replied that she would go wherever I decided to go. Two days later I was called for an interview and a month later I had a job offer to go to work for Roan Consolidated Mines Ltd., a copper mining company in Zambia. My expatriate package was attractive and offered opportunity to save for the future. I made a commitment to go away for a period of three years.

We decided to sell our house and mentioned it to friends of ours. Next day there was a knock on the door. It was a man who had heard that we were selling our house; his wife was expecting a baby and they were desperately looking for a place to get away from an intolerant landlord. He inspected the house, fell in love with it and expressed willingness to buy it, providing the price was reasonable. I told him the price. It was what I had paid for it. We shook hands and set the process of transfer of ownership in motion.

I then believed that morally I had no right to profit from the sale of that house as I was there for less than five years and had made no value-adding changes to the property. Moreover, I was already a beneficiary of the noble act of the previous owner. Any profiteering at the expense of the new buyer, who was as desperate for a house as I had been, was not going to make me very rich, and very likely not proud of myself either. No estate agent was involved. I had already formed my opinion, right or wrong, about estate agents who practise aspirational pricing to earn more commissions. The process escalates property prices without creating any additional wealth.

To this day in my very simplistic, and possibly naïve in the eyes of many people, way of thinking, I have not come to grips with the notion that a residential property should escalate in value and make the owner a real capital gain over a period of time. We live in a world claiming to be so civilised that it recognises every individual's moral right to have shelter in addition to clothing, food and employment. Why should it then become more and more difficult for young people, buying their first house, to afford it? Property price escalations are effectively a means of taking a dividend out of future earnings of the new purchaser of an existing property. The new purchasers undertake this burden in the hope that they will also be able to extract a dividend out of someone's future.

The social system creates an environment which dictates that you are only secure in your society if you own your house. The economic monetary and fiscal policies allow qualifying individuals to borrow money to buy and own a home. Looking at it rather cynically I cannot help saying if one has borrowed money to buy a house and will now spend a substantial part of his or her working life to repay the loan with interest, the individual does not own his or her house; rather it is the house that owns the individual.

I am baffled by a culture that says that you may have what you desire, within limits of course, but then you must toil hard to repay the debt you have created. On the lending side of the equation there can be layers upon layers of complex and multi-faceted financing schemes and instruments for a number of institutions and individuals to rake off advance dividends in the guise of charges, commissions and bonuses. This is their preoccupation.

When easy credit is available, enterprising individuals are lured into investing borrowed money in property to rent out such that the income pays the debt and passage of time creates a capital gain from rise in value of the property. Ironically over the lifetime of the tenant the ownership of the property may change hands a number of times and every time this happens, the amount of money that changes hands increases, yet the total space offered by the property, and the purpose it serves, remain the same. Such gains can only be illusory beyond a certain limit and can only be sustained as long as there are chains of lenders available to lend money.

When individuals, disproportionately large in number, rely upon such ephemeral schemes for existence, an unfavourable jolt to the economic process can cause immense hardship. Tenants may fail to pay rent due to unemployment or high interest rates or general inflation, and as a result landlords may default on their obligations to their lenders, and the declining property values may force the lenders to demand equity reinstatement on borrowers. The entire chain is destabilised causing all the middlemen to fall, but the property remains intact, which only demonstrates that all the gains were only mythical.

What is real survives.

Property owners thrive on a sense of perceived wealth measured by illusory gains based on valuations placed on them by parties with self-interest. When these valuations do not generate further propulsion of the cycle, the sense of perceived wealth becomes a sense of impending impoverishment, and thus a source of misery.

Certainly in my case I felt as if I was a captive of my property, my first major asset. I was becoming too possessive about it but found care and maintenance of it beyond my capability. Attending to minor chores like small water leaks, dripping taps and peeled wallpapers was not something I cherished. Fixing the cistern in the toilet or finding out why the central heating was not working were major challenges for me. It hurt my pride having to solicit help from a friend or a relative and calling a tradesman to attend to these problems was out of the question for fear of being ripped off.

Still under thirty, I truly felt relieved like never before upon disposal of this house which felt more like a ball and chain round my ankle rather than a home.

In less than ten years I had gained a professional qualification without failing a single examination, got married, started a family, had a house, a good job and a company car - everything I needed to demonstrate to the society that I was a successful man. *"Why do I have to prove anything to the society?" "And what next?" "What is my true purpose in life?"*

On the inside I was lacking a real sense of satisfaction and joy. Something true was missing. All that I had achieved so far, if I can call it an achievement, was only my accumulations and credentials, a mere show that I was no less than anyone else – a reaction to my perceived opinions of others about me. *"For how long can I live a merely reactive life?"* This question was hounding me.

EIGHT

Return To Africa

It was nearly ten years since I first set foot in Britain, but I was still reeling from blows dealt on my psyche in the past. Coming to Zambia in Southern Africa was another major turning point in my life. In many ways it felt as if I had returned home to my roots to regain lost orientation. It may sound a little oxymoronic, but fate took me back to Africa to start a process in me of putting behind and forgetting the childhood and teenage life experiences in Uganda. There was a deep inexplicable sense of ease and self-assuredness that I had not experienced in my previous ten years in Britain. I guess I had become slightly disillusioned with the life in the West. The Zambian air and atmosphere gave me a sense of déjà vu.

As I reflect upon the time when the decision to go to Zambia had been made, I distinctly remember that I had no apprehension about going to that unfamiliar territory or any second thoughts or doubt about my decision. This was no routine step in life and I, only I, was responsible for this decision. No one in the family, including my in-laws, tried to talk me out of it. My father-in-law, who had been deprived of his property through nationalisation by the Tanzanian Government, was one person who might have had a good reason to dissuade me. But he did not stand in my way. Even the fact that my own family was very young, two sons - younger one, Rushi, only three months old and the elder one, Nick, just under three years at the time of our departure – did not deter me or Umi from embarking on this venture. Deep within I had a feeling of confidence and self-assurance that I was marching in the direction of my dreams. Something told me that everything would work out well. And so we arrived in Zambia.

Previously known as Northern Rhodesia, Zambia, boasting a population of ten million, became independent in October 1964 and has been known as a peaceful country, rich in agriculture, wildlife and minerals like copper, lead, zinc, silver and cobalt. The discovery of the minerals, mainly copper and cobalt, was made in the late 1920s which dramatically changed Zambia's fate. By 1939 Zambia had become potentially a very rich country as it had become the world's largest producer of copper. The country also boasted large deposits of precious and semi-precious stones like emeralds, rubies and sapphires, and thus offered itself to pioneering exploiters.

Europeans, mainly from Britain, found the land to be attractive from economic, climatic, political and social viewpoints. By 1955, the whites numbered more than 50,000 and constituted in excess of 3% of the total population. Here they enjoyed a higher standard of living than in post-war Britain – a white worker earned on average £2,070 a year compared to his black counterpart who made £203 a year. During this pre-independence period about the only major development to have been achieved in Zambia was the Kariba dam, built to produce hydroelectricity.

Under their first President, Dr. Kenneth David Kaunda, the people of Zambia inherited from the British a healthy balance of payments surplus and a sizeable foreign currency reserve. Against this the country could lamentably only boast a few dozen indigenous graduates and only a relatively small number of primary and secondary schools.

During the first ten years of independence the country suffered the same fate as any other African country had done post independence: massive inflation, unchecked state spending and borrowing to fulfil promises made to the people to provide schools, hospitals and employment. Key industries were nationalised, which as a result inhibited foreign investment and spurred exodus of expatriate skills. The country's economic mainstay was still copper. The world prices of this commodity had fallen in real terms and concurrently the price of oil, Zambia's major import, had rocketed. Not surprisingly there was scarcity of foreign exchange which forced the Government to restrict importation of certain non-essential items. Consequently, many luxuries and a number of essential household items became scarce or disappeared from once thriving shops.

In the opinion of many commentators some of the economic hardships had been self-imposed, in that President Kaunda ran a manifesto to support the Southern Rhodesian Africans' struggle for independence from Mr. Ian Smith's administration which had formed an alliance with the apartheid regime of South Africa for its sustenance as the country faced economic sanctions from all leading economies of the world after its Unilateral Declaration of Independence. Southern Rhodesia later became Zimbabwe. The UDI was Ian Smith's measure to prevent Britain from handing the country to the majority African population and to maintain the security and supremacy of the white minority population that had lived there for several generations.

Zambia is a landlocked country and has always had to depend on the ports of neighbouring countries for its imports and exports. Dr. Kaunda, in support of the sanctions, stopped using the southern corridor for the country's trade and opted to use the more expensive and inefficient Tanzanian port of Dar-es-Salaam. The application of trade sanctions against Southern Rhodesia and South Africa did more damage than good to Zambia as the country had to not only make use of the Dar port, but also import raw materials, capital goods, key industrial inputs, medicines and several other critical items over longer distances from Europe and Japan as opposed to South Africa, its cheapest and nearest source of most supplies that came by road and rail.

In order to truly appreciate the extent of the self-inflicted hardship suffered by Zambia to support the trade sanctions, it is necessary to understand that in spite of the fact that the Zambian mining industry infrastructure, methods and culture were closely intertwined with those of their South African and Southern Rhodesian counterparts, Zambia chose to import essential spares and components for critical South African manufactured mining equipment like locomotives, pumps, crushers, dump trucks, loaders and so on from Europe and the USA, and where necessary, modified the equipment at a high cost for compatibility with the spares and components from Europe.

As a mark of solidarity with the independence movement, the country also provided refuge to Joshua Nkomo's liberation army. Nkomo was the nationalist leader of the Zimbabwe African Peoples Union. It was said in some quarters then that Dr. Kaunda was taking these measures in the hope that a subsequent economic pact with independent Zimbabwe would rescue Zambia from her economic woes. History took a different course thereafter in that Joshua Nkomo surrendered power to Robert Mugabe, and what disaster befell independent Zimbabwe is well documented.

I arrived in Zambia, to work as an expatriate in the mines, three years before Southern Rhodesia became Zimbabwe and Robert Mugabe took the reigns. The country was in turmoil. It was against this backdrop that I left peaceful and relatively thriving Great Britain. Irrational, irresponsible and reckless as it may have appeared to a sound mind, I had proceeded with the intent to migrate because deep down I had a feeling that I would take a liking to Zambia and find in that country my kind of joyful existence.

I was posted at one of the oldest copper and cobalt

mines in a town called Luanshya, described in the colonial days as the garden city of the Copperbelt, a province renowned for rich mineral deposits. Like all the major Zambian towns, Luanshya had been designed and built to reflect the segregationist policies of the old colonial days. There were the first class and second class trading areas for Europeans and everyone else respectively. Similarly there were the more salubrious residential housing areas for the whites and then a grade or two lower area for the Indians and other races, and finally very congested low-cost structures and shanty compounds for the blacks. The African township was built in the direction of the prevailing wind which took with it all the acidic fumes from the smelters. Generally the high-cost housing areas for the whites were the most developed with spacious detached houses and beautifully laid lawns along tree-lined avenues.

The Zambian towns were planned and built in the colonial times by the British to cater for much smaller populations than did actually inhabit them in the post-colonial period. Consequently, there were serious housing, water, electricity and sewerage problems, particularly in the Asian and African townships.

Whereas sporting and social life was wonderful, I could not say the same for my work. Amongst nearly twenty expatriate accountants at Luanshya, I was the only Chartered Accountant with the most recent City of London experience but my position was so junior that I was merely involved in clerical work of the kind I would have performed as an articled clerk in my days of training. My only consolation was that my contract was only for a period of three years at the end of which I would return home with significant savings. This would enable a comfortable resettlement back in England for me and my family. I managed to persuade myself to stay put and suffer the humiliation, but this was only for a few months after which I seriously began considering breaking my contract and returning home but just could not make up my mind. Not being happy at all, I made my feelings known to the Financial Controller who appreciated that I was much overqualified for the position I was holding, but he had nothing to offer other than to remind me to think about the financial implications of breaking my contract.

Notwithstanding this, resigning appeared to be a better option for my conscience than to take home a salary every month and remit a third of it into my bank account in the UK. I began to say to myself, *"I am grossly overpaid at the expense of basically the people of a poor nation. I cannot be a party to a process that is not noble. I cannot take what I have not truly earned. My job can be easily done by a*

Zambian clerk at about the tenth of the cost". My resignation letter was ready to go.

Just then a shocking incident took place in town – the wife of one of my senior expatriate colleagues died after being shot in a robbery incident. He was naturally away for several weeks. During his absence, in a series of acting promotions to fill the gap, I found myself moving up one notch and doing a reasonably responsible job which exposed me to several mining engineers. I held back my resignation letter and finally tore it up when I was confirmed as Departmental Accountant - Mining upon resignation of my bereaved colleague who had to return to England for the sake of his young children.

I am saddened to note that it was the unfortunate death of a perfectly innocent woman that brought about a major change in my career. Nature truly works in strange ways but it has a purpose hidden in every one of its quirks.

I began to make a favourable impression on my superiors, and so in a subsequent spate of expatriate departures on account of poor security, I was favoured to fill a position two ranks higher as a Management Accountant. I was now truly in a position to demonstrate my capabilities and soon became quite popular amongst senior managers of the Division.

I have no guilt feelings about not showing solidarity with the returning expatriates who left on the grounds of security, simply because I was aware at the outset that such was a major concern in the country and every expatriate was an obvious target of armed thugs coming from the neighbouring Zaïre, a country bankrupted by the despotic Mobutu's regime which even failed to pay salaries to its soldiers, thus leaving them to fend for themselves. Atrocities committed by these stray soldiers and other thugs brought much fear and distress to the residents of all the major towns of the Copperbelt. Each family was essentially responsible for its own safety, the local police guards being under-resourced and not suitably trained to combat such crime.

Wealthy individuals were the prime targets of these robbers who took from them motor vehicles, cash and jewellery at gunpoint. They hurt and killed those who resisted. Such robberies and killings became commonplace. Although the mines set up armed patrols with their own licensed police and sealed off roads at night to restrict entry and exit points, where security personnel were posted all night, there was very little they could do to curb highway robberies. This situation affected the lives of all, expatriates and others alike. Many remained confined in-house after work and in the weekends, their main purpose being to work and repatriate savings to their home countries whilst their contracts lasted. Those nearing the date of expiry of their relatively lucrative contracts had an equal concern and contract renewal gave them immense relief.

Every expatriate and non-Zambian resident had their own agenda for living in Zambia in spite of the obvious frustrations emanating from the prevailing insecurity, shortages of essential commodities, poor roads and rampant corruption. And I was only interested in my agenda. The question I asked myself was, *'Why am I putting up with all this?'*

Was I greedy? Did I simply like the easy life? Was I selfish?

At some point in time the answer to each of these questions may have been *'yes'*, but I was not proud of that. I had to put matters right. I had been there for about two years during which time I had made a mark as a cricketer. Cricket was played in the dry cool months of April to September. But this was just a colonial hangover. Was it doing anything for an indigenous Zambian? No it wasn't, and yet the National Sports Council was most accommodating in allowing cricket, not only to be dominated by foreigners, but the foreigners were also allowed to represent the national team and given generous cash allowances to meet the cost of travelling out of Zambia to play in international events. Cricket became my major livelihood. It led me to playing racquet squash and golf also.

Thus sport was a major attraction for me. I was a beneficiary of the good nature of the Zambian people. I was good enough to be selected for the Zambian national cricket squad and for a number of years represented the national team in the Southern and Central African regional tournament, not only as a player, but also as vice-captain and later as team coach. I was also fortunate enough to have been selected in the East and Central African squad to participate in the ICC Trophy. Over the years I had the pleasure of playing against the likes of John Hampshire, Mark Nicholas, David Houghton, Ramnath Parker and many other renowned cricketers.

In spite of the overhanging poor security situation and the frustrations of not having some of the smaller luxuries of living in England, my family and I had begun to feel reasonably comfortable and made several friends. It was easy to make friends with other expatriates and local Indians as we all shared the same concerns. The expatriate social life apart from sport involved dinners and parties. There was just too much of the good life and the danger that one was becoming too indulgent in it.

Just then another promotion landed on my doorstep. This led to relocation to Kalulushi, a small mining town where I was now assistant Financial Controller. Being further away from the border with Zaire, this cul-de-sac town enjoyed a relatively better security. My work was now of a truly responsible nature and I felt myself making a contribution, both at divisional and corporate level. My experience was now being properly put to a test. I sat on various committees which involved interaction with my counterparts at the other divisions and the Head Office. I came to be noticed by the more senior officials of the company, giving me immense job satisfaction. For the first time a realisation dawned on me that I was now earning my salary and helping to improve lives of others.

To me improving the lives of others firstly meant transferring my skills to my indigenous Zambian colleagues and sincerely promoting Zambianisation. The policy of Zambianisation had been receiving only lip service because the entrenched expatriate order had self-interest at heart. It was understandable though. Human nature being what it is, long-serving expatriates, having given their lives to Zambia and fearing they were unemployable in their own countries, preferred to remain in Zambia until they were ready financially to retire. Consequently, they did not truly commit to the idea of Zambianisation, and so the whole process was frustrating for many young, willing, able and keen Zambians.

At a personal level I had to address this matter. Clearly the idea that a country has to spend foreign currency for an imported basic resource, like a mechanic or a laboratory technician, when local skills could be trained and hired for only a fraction of the cost was unpalatable to me. *How can a country be so reliant on basic foreign skills after nearly two decades of independence?* I wholeheartedly began to subscribe to accelerated training and placement of Zambians in positions becoming vacant after expiry of expatriate contracts. *"If this means even I would be working myself out of a job, then so be it"*, I used to repeat to myself.

In many ways this ideal was more appropriate for me to carry. At a deeper level I liked and admired the Zambian people. Most of the town dwellers, and all those I came in contact with in my daily life, spoke English - I am ashamed to say that in my seventeen years in Zambia, I did not learn to speak any of their languages - I found them to be humble and respectful, but proud people. In contrast to the Ugandans, they did not have the aggressive streak in them, or hostility towards foreigners. I found them to be a nation of generally God fearing, peaceful and very kind people. They deserved prosperity and progress.

Some of the old guard who grew up in the colonial times were greatly disillusioned by the economic state of their nation which they fought hard to free from their colonial masters. They were particularly resentful of their modern day leaders who tried to explain the economic woes as a temporary, but inevitable, consequence of independence. I recall being told of what one elderly village headman once said in a reminiscing mood after recounting the good old colonial days when there was plenty of work, no food and water shortages, security was good, tribalism was not heard of and there was no inflation. He concluded his sad lament with the words, *"I don't know when this independence is going to come to an end".*

Whilst I was firmly entrenched in my work, I was becoming aware that my first contract was soon expiring. Would I be happy to return to the UK if I was not offered a renewal? Fortunately I was offered another three year stint.

I sought promotion of Zambian interest in all walks of life, including sport. One day I noticed that a sixteen year-old schoolboy playing squash with other boys had a special talent which could not go unnoticed. In my capacity as a committee member of the club I invited him to join the practice sessions with the seniors, comprising mainly expatriates. There was some resistance initially on the grounds that he was too young to play with men and to travel to play league matches. These were feeble reasons to keep locals infiltrating an expatriates' domain.

However, this was soon forgotten as Philip became accepted as a young member of the team. And I was completely vindicated when he progressed in the Copperbelt from playing fifth in the 'C' league to playing first in the 'A' league in his first season at the club. He became the first indigenous Zambian to win the national championship before he was twenty. Subsequently, he was sent on a squash scholarship to the UK and on returning became the Southern African regional champion. This was the beginning of Zambianisation of squash which continued unabated thereafter. Philip is now known as a Zambian squash legend.

Unfortunately, the same could not be achieved with cricket which is slow, lengthy and riddled with rituals. Zambians found it rather strange, but the real inhibitor was finance. Cricket, being expensive, did not hold much appeal for them. A pair of cricket shoes cost an equivalent of an average Zambian's weekly salary. Everything about the game was out of their reach.

My greatest satisfaction came from being involved with Zambians at grass roots level. Helping, developing and motivating young talent created a sense of fulfilment. Some, who had enterprise in them, needed help to set up small businesses in market stalls, some needed help with further education and some with housing or transport. I have no desire to elaborate on what I may have done for the needy, nor do I, I am glad to state, remember any specific instances in depth. These were not favours, simply a duty that any decent human being would perform.

What I may have done for any indigenous people of Zambia was nothing unique. Indeed, there were many like me, and some foreigners even dedicated their entire lives to the betterment of Zambia. As I look back, I know I had no expectations of any kind of return for these acts.

If you love your job, do not allow the thought of losing it enter your mind. I always reminded myself that I was only on a three-year contract which could be terminated at three month's notice. I would have been willing to leave on being told my services were no longer needed by the mining industry. Meanwhile my purpose was to remain aligned with Zambia and the Zambian people in their strife to improve conditions.

As it happened, my contract kept on being renewed. I had to address the implications of returning to the UK after a prolonged stay abroad. I feared it would not be possible for me to enter the mainstream accounting and finance field upon returning as I was totally out of touch with all new developments. I resigned to the idea that I would be unemployable in the UK on my return, and thought no more about it.

A series of promotions at work took me away from the drudgeries of accounting and finance to integration of the mining industry, strategy formation, working on ad-hoc committees, development of new management style, training and development, diversification of the national economy from dependency on mining to agriculture and tourism, and ultimately to transformation of the mining enterprise from a parastatal to private ownership. I found myself collaborating with officials from the World Bank, the IMF, some consulting firms like Andersen Consulting and SRI and similar organisations – all concerned with improving the country's economy.

First and foremost it was necessary to have a deeper and broader understanding of the state Zambia was in and why. The economic and financial trauma of attempts to fulfil aspirations of the masses in the pre-independence period had to be understood, evaluated and stage managed. Their tribal and traditional differences, every Zambian's general, or perceived, allegiance with and inclination towards his or her own tribe and mistrust of other tribes had to be given due deference in formulating any fiscal, economic and social policies. Rural and rustic Zambians were accustomed to the guidance and control exercised by their President and the One Party Democracy Rule. He was respected for his philosophy of Humanism which put man at the centre of everything. The people of Zambia were accustomed to the manner in which he had first and foremost brought tribal balancing in the affairs of the state for more than two decades and held the nation together in peace. There were price controls on staple food and essential items to protect the poor.

The country was beset with problems caused both by factors within its control and outside its control. The external factors included high oil prices, historically low copper prices, drought that forced the country to import maize and refugee infiltration due to the unrest in the neighbouring Angola, Mozambique and Zimbabwe. The local councils of all the major towns could not maintain basic amenities, roads, water supply, sewerage treatment, medical facilities and schools through lack of finance and technical skills. The problems were compounded by migration of young aspiring Zambians from villages to towns. Crime was rampant.

The run-down state of the infrastructure called for massive capital injection in the country and support of specialist skills to put matters right. Over the years the State had already built a portfolio of loans from developed countries which it was not able to repay. After much pleading, major reconstruction loans and aid were made available by donor nations and the IMF, but on conditions. These conditions called for, amongst other things, liberalisation of imports, relaxation of import duties, abolition of price and foreign exchange controls, the local currency, kwacha, to be floated in the open market, privatisation of the mining industry and introduction of multi-party democracy. These were unpalatable conditions, but beggars cannot be choosers unfortunately. These impositions touched the heart and soul of the whole nation. These biting conditions began to be implemented.

When the multi-party election date was set and campaigns began, many expatriates feared a backlash from the Kaunda faithfuls if he did not win. It was rumoured that the army would takeover and there would be a bloodbath. There was so much fear that many expatriates sent their families back home, fortified their houses against looters and filled their pantries with essential requirements. Some armed themselves with guns and other weapons. There was little outdoor life, and intense tension and anxiety.

I was reminded of the Idi Amin days in Uganda and told to take precautions by some friends and acquaintances. This was a real test of character. I asked myself *'Do I simply love the money I am paid, or am I really loyal to Zambia?'*, *'Do I not regard the Zambians as peaceful and compassionate people any more?'*, *'How can I appear as if I have forsaken them in their hour of greatest need of goodwill?'* I could not bear the thought of being selfish and indifferent. Zambia and the Zambians had given me a home. I remained optimistic and continued life as normal.

President Kaunda was defeated by Mr Chiluba, a trade unionist. He bowed out gracefully and multi-party democracy was ushered in peacefully. This may have been a defeat for the old guard but a victory for the whole nation for the manner in which it conducted itself in the eyes of the whole world. I felt vindicated in my resolve to stay put; faith that all would work out well having prevailed. Zambia taught me to develop faith in the inner spirit and to place full trust in it when all else appears to be failing. I never had any serious personal security concerns, for I had immersed myself fully in one purpose, and that was to exercise my best endeavours in the process to make Zambia a better country.

I was witness to all changes in the country which its people accepted with an open mind knowing that a great deal of turmoil and hardship were in the offing. Prices began to rise as the national currency started to lose value on the open market. There was no shortage of maize flour but a fair market price had to be paid.

Zambia had embraced change and was ready for the challenges lying ahead. It takes a great deal of grit and fortitude to bow to impositions of this magnitude from outsiders whose own various Western economic models have not been proven to run successfully without causing mass cyclical upheavals and distress.

In all, within the mining industry, Zambia gave me opportunities to bring meaning to my life. There was a deep sense of self-worth coming from a knowing that whatever I did in my own limited way was intended firstly to serve the interest of its people, and then mine. I like to believe that I learnt to reach out to other people empathetically, to appreciate other cultures and to strive to eliminate prejudice. Prejudice is a poison that lurks deep inside one's self, and slowly and systematically chisels away at one's soul.

I was able to live in Zambia the kind of life I had imagined, as a youth, for myself in Uganda. This was a seventeen year period of enriching experience and sheer joy. There was something in the Zambian air that made me feel at home. Unfortunately I had to return to the UK.

I was diagnosed with glaucoma. Glaucoma is an eye condition in which the optic nerve is irreparably damaged at the point where it leaves the eye. This nerve carries information from the light sensitive layer in the eye, the retina, to the brain where it is perceived as a picture. An eye needs a certain amount of pressure to keep the eyeball in shape so that it can work properly. In some people, the damage is caused by raised eye pressure. Others may have an eye pressure within normal limits, but damage occurs because there is a weakness in the optic nerve. In most cases both factors are involved to a varying degree. This eye pressure is not generally related to blood pressure, but the damage results in impaired vision. With surgery the pressure can be relieved, but excessive glare of artificial light and strong sunlight can cause much discomfort.

My doctors were of the view that an appropriate level of medical care for my condition was not available in Zambia and I should decide what was best for me and my family.

All good things have to come to an end. There is a sound note to the conclusion of this wonderful phase of my life – an elderly Zambian office messenger made a remark to me as a parting gesture which when translated meant, *"as worthy as the prize-winning bull in the agriculture show"*. I love Zambia and her wonderful people!

NINE

GIFT FROM ZAMBIA

Nature reciprocates. Its ways are mysterious. It does things when they are least expected. It gives what is right and appropriate. What happened one day at work in my office, still in Zambia, long before my return to England, ushered in the beginning of a major, but gradual, constructive change in my life. It opened up a whole new world, brought a new dynamic force into my spiritual and psychic constitution and changed the way I now perceive life's hidden dimensions. It has put me in a state of eternal gratitude and set me on a discovery path. I began to enjoy spells of being in a vibrant world of tranquillity and bliss.

It was said by many long-serving expatriates that to enter Zambia was child's play but to leave Zambia was almost impossible because of cumbersome and lengthy emigration formalities. A fellow employee I will call BR, an Indian expatriate, walked into my office. He was in his mid-fifties, well-built and very energetic, but carrying the clean-shaven face of a kind-hearted man. The glow on his face exuded fatherly love. He sat down and placed a pile of papers on my desk. He said he was leaving Zambia after several years and wanted advice on how he should go about dealing with his repatriation formalities. He had not been able to handle matters himself. For family and financial reasons, it was necessary for him to leave by a certain date. He had already booked himself on a flight out to India.

I examined his papers and employment history and regretted that unfortunately it was not going to be possible for him to fly out of Zambia at his desired time. I knew this meant a deep frustration and a huge financial loss to him. I was not certain how he would react.

In essence what had transpired was that his contract had come to an end and he was required to vacate the company house within a certain period. His flight to India had been paid for. All his money from local savings, sale of household items and end of contract gratuity was frozen in his bank account, waiting to be externalised. My vague recollection is that he was out of work, would soon have no money, he was about to be homeless and not able to leave Zambia for at least three months. In brief, he would be stranded like a refugee. This would disrupt all his future plans and his airfare was not refundable if he did not take his flight on the scheduled date.

This was a unique situation and BR was receiving no sympathy from the Emigration Officers. His guilt was that he did not follow a proper repatriation procedure. The situation was frustrating enough to anger anyone, but not BR. He sat quietly in contemplation for a few moments and then taking a deep breath of relief, said he would leave the problem in the hands of his Master, and let things take their own course.

I was taken aback by his, what I then regarded as a, fatalistic attitude to this very serious matter. *"In the hands of the Master?"* I quizzed him. He said in a highly reassured voice, *"Yes, my spiritual Master, who guides me and opens up a door for me whenever I am troubled. I simply say what I want and leave the rest to him"*. I sat back eager to listen to him as he perked up and started to assume command of our meeting. He was clearly dedicated to his Master and had no doubt that all would work out. The self-assuredness he derived from his belief in a spiritual force was stunning. I could not believe how anyone could have so much faith.

He spoke about an ancient science of soul travel called Eckankar, a means by which inner consciousness is projected into the higher realms of existence, for the experience of total awareness of being, through meditative and contemplative exercises. It is a system of experiencing light and sound, the primordial elements, as a way of gaining all teachings emanating from the divine source, or God. It is the primal source, the origin, of all religions. Its teachings guide us to recognize the presence of the Holy Spirit in our lives. We learn that each of us is Soul, a spark of God sent to this world to gain spiritual experiences. And as we unfold spiritually, we learn to express the love of God through service to others. For centuries the knowledge of Eckankar had been passed down through oral tutelage to all who were ready for it, until 1965 when Sri Paul Twitchell, as the spiritual head of Eckankar, started to bring the teachings to the world through books, lectures and writings. Paulji, as he was known as to all his disciples, was a student, a chela, of a teacher in India, who trained him to become a living Eck Master.

This was my formal introduction to spirituality in my mid-thirties. I met BR several times thereafter. He unhesitatingly welcomed me to his house and spoke about Eckankar for hours. The understanding and practice of the knowledge of Eckankar passed on to me by BR began to become my aide and ally in all my endeavours. As I read about Eckankar and attended a few workshops, it began to appear to me that this was the purest, unadulterated form of Hinduism – or, for that matter, any of the established religions, being the source of all religions. This is what attracted me most to Eckankar – that it embraced all religions and its followers were not dissuaded from following their religion of birth or choice. Most Eckists and aspirants I met expressed some dissatisfaction with their religion of birth and looked for a path that answered some fundamental questions without compelling them to conform.

I felt at home with what I read about Eckankar. The early discourses I studied became a catalyst in enabling my understanding of spirituality. Until then my belief in the higher force was based on loosely woven notions which I was always hesitant to share with anyone. I was now beginning to follow a path that made a great deal of sense to me and answered one fundamental question I had harboured for a long time – *'Why are religions divisive?'* Calling myself a Hindu meant I was not a Moslem or a Christian or a Sikh or a Jew or a Buddhist or of any other religious denomination for that matter. There was so much good in every religion, and yet calling myself a Hindu meant denying myself the privilege of being cosseted by, and experiencing, the sweet nectar of all other religions. The little that I have learnt from my observations, Hinduism is about connectedness with everything and how to manifest one's own reality. Islam is about self knowledge, unquestioned devotion to Allah, humility and common decency. Christianity espouses charity, compassion and love. Buddhism provides gateway to self-realisation and serenity. Similarly every other religion has a something unique in store for a seeker.

Eckankar, being all-embracing, answered the question. It tells me to live in a world of invisible realities and teaches me that my spiritual growth is totally in my hands - I am responsible for everything that happens to me.

The five passions, lust, anger, greed, attachment and vanity are expounded upon at length in Eckankar, and as I became aware of these in my daily life, it became apparent to me that they are a millstone hung around my neck - the chief hindrances to real happiness and true spiritual growth.

Just as free radicals, the debilitating oxygen molecules floating in our blood stream and depriving healthy molecules of their energy, are by-products of the various processes of the body and come from external sources such as environmental and chemical toxins, passions are the debilitating virtual molecules in our spirit which come from our social and psychic pickling. Until identified and recognised as polluting toxins hindering the expansion of our spirit, they continue to keep us from truly realising ourselves.

We are all possessed by these perversions of the mind. Our social conditioning is the chief architect of these perversions, which create a false sense of external reality and thus mask the underlying ignorance of self. These passions are the real enemy within.

Spirituality, as I understand it, is a state of being in which one feels the presence of the divine force in every act one performs. There is recognition that all of one's thoughts, emotions, words and actions are guided by the divine force. There is a total alignment of the physical, psychic, emotional and spiritual states in a continuum. Very simply, it means waking up and truly experiencing the beauty of, not only human, but all existence. It is all about spirit, a unifying force that pervades all religions and theological beliefs.

One of the offerings of spirituality is a heightened sense of awareness in which a person remains poised to soar in all directions. Hidden dimensions become apparent. One's imagination ceases to know any bonds.

Nothing becomes insurmountable. A person's thoughts break all shackles put on him by years of limiting conditioning. Social and religious norms have no purchase on such a person.

I see established religion and spirituality as:

- Religion is a man-made concept with a firm set of precepts, dogmas and ideologies. Spirituality is a spontaneous reaction to life.

- Religion is stamped on an individual at birth and can be changed to another faith and learned through tutelage. Spirituality is realised through experiences, perhaps over several lifetimes.

- Religion is based on spirituality, and is in it. Spirituality does not need religion.

- Religion can become binding. Spirituality is liberating.

- Religion mostly identifies with rituals and place of worship. Spirituality demands no rituals, and does not need any place of worship.

- Religion may be identified with a founder,

seeks identity and separates itself from other religions. Spirituality is awakening of the self. It is all embracing and not given or taught.

• Religion, through egoist misinterpretations, becomes divisive in its end result. Spirituality is unifying and integrating.

Highly spiritual individuals, having lived and learned through many lifetimes, are awake in the true sense of the word, and alive to the core. Driven by love and compassion, not any religious dogma, they are pure consciousness. They do not need to wear any religious coating for they are Christlike, not Christians, Buddhalike, not Buddhists, so to speak. They live by their acquired skill of being, which is a divine function of the soul, rather than simply a doing which is a physical act of the body. Being decisive, they act with a clear sense of purpose, and serve it with an unwavering and consistent zest. They walk like they talk, and talk like they walk. In serving their purpose they do not discern between good and evil, rich and poor, or any religious and social labels. They act without prejudice or judgement in the fashion of the Arab saying, *"the nature of rain is the same, but it makes thorns grow in the marshes, and flowers in the gardens"*. Being largely devoid of judgement, they see no divisions, no barriers, no national boundaries or borders, but simply a universe of limitless existence which is full of mysteries about life.

I returned to England with a novitiate's understanding of spirituality, and far less concern for self and how others would see me. I had begun to overcome sensitivity to the opinions of others. When uninvited opinions of others, good or bad, cease to make a difference, real avenues of growth and lasting prosperity begin to open up. Unrestricted and unbounded an individual becomes fearless in the face of challenges, perceives no obstacles, nor cares about being branded as a failure.

TEN

A NEW BEGINNING

"The poverty in the west is a different kind of poverty

– it's not only poverty of loneliness, but also of spirituality"

Mother Teresa

As anticipated, I was unemployable in the UK on a kind of salary and status I was accustomed to in Zambia. It was during my search for occupation of some kind that I was persuaded by a practising accountant, a fellow Patel from my own town in Uganda and origins in my ancestral village in India, to invest in a manufacturing project in India. He was promoting this for KSB, a Sikh enterprising-sounding individual from Slough, Berkshire in England, but with influential relations in, and familiarity with, India.

I parted with a large proportion of my savings and became a shareholder-director of a newly-formed company. Little did I know then that this venture was about to open a whole new facet of understanding of life and human nature for me. It has been a test of my character and major trigger in changing my self-awareness and thought process, which have both been instrumental in taking me towards a fulfilling life.

A few weeks after our factory was opened, the first shipment of production arrived in England and was sold, followed by another soon. The project appeared to have made a promising start. But, a few months later, it began to become apparent that the rate of production was not living up to forecast, causing concern to the contract customers and the bank. In the wake of this situation, I went to India.

To my horror, the project was not what it was made to look like. The amount of money invested by me and from the bank loan did not appear to have been all spent in setting up the factory. I sensed fraud and reported this to Mr Patel, the man behind persuading me - and the bank - into parting with our monies.

In the ensuing months of turmoil, KSB disappeared somewhere in India, leaving his wife and young children stranded in England, penniless. It transpired that he had also borrowed money from his mother-in-law. My further enquiries revealed that he had previously been jailed for fraud in England. In a nutshell, it proved Mr Patel's incompetence and failure to carry out proper due diligence. It turned out later that Patel had let down many of his clients, mainly ex-Ugandans. Not many Asians had kind words to say about him. Scores lost their hard earned savings in his fiendish snares. He finally got his comeuppance when the Institute of Chartered Accountants struck him off for conduct unbecoming of a professional accountant. Apart from losing my investment, I ended up paying off the bank loan.

Thus began my return to England with this debacle, involving a man from my own ancestral village in India who was therefore a distant cousin with whom I had an immediate affinity. Naturally, I was devastated and distraught. Betrayal of trust hurts. My dream to give my family a nice home and a comfortable life in England had been shattered, as indeed my spirit. My initiative to go along with Patel's idea was based on trust in fellow Chartered Accountants and the ambition to be involved in some kind of manufacture.

My naïveté was clear from the choice of people to associate with and my trusting disposition. I guess this was mainly from seventeen years of having no experience of 'sharks' in Zambia. For too long I had been accustomed to dealing with people on trust at a personal level. I truly began to appreciate what a wonderful community of people I had lived with in Zambia.

KSB's wife was distraught and angry too. She wanted him to be found and brought to justice. In one conversation she said she and her son wanted '*his head on a platter*' and could not believe why I was so placid after being duped out of so much money. My answer then was, and even now is, '*He will be living in fear and looking over his shoulder all his life. A man who has to fear his own son has gone nowhere and gained nothing in life. His fear will stymie everything he tries to do in life. This is his sentence.*'

We do not have to live in the past, for the past holds us back. A man with a deep sense of wrongdoing cannot forget his past, for he is constantly striving to forget it. As he tries to forget it, his mind remains preoccupied with trying to forget it and so it remains fresh in his mind to haunt him. He has no present, merely a past to bury, which keeps cropping up like weeds in an untended garden. Such a person can never look in the mirror and be proud of what he sees.

My experience with these two individuals gave me a good measure of myself, in a relative sense, and affirmed the kind of person I am not, and never will be. I have no wish to condemn, nor hate either of them. If I allowed the incident to touch me, I would surrender power to it. This would then prevent me from coming out of the mire of suffering. This was not suffering, merely an experience.

Suffering is just a notion, or a negative interpretation of a state one is in. I cannot place blame on anyone if I chose to interpret a situation as a failure or suffering, and if I do, it can only be my fault. The words of Dada Bhagwan, an enlightened Gujarati soul, are most fitting, *"the fault is always of the sufferer"*. I chose not to be a sufferer.

There are so many people who always dwell on the negative and blame someone or something for their failures. If no-one in particular can be blamed, it is the Higher Force to blame for what happens to them without understanding that the basic quality of the creative force, the Nature, is to nurture our growth.

The way to live in the positive state is to understand and live by the adage 'everything that happens, happens for the best' and has a purpose sown within it. The thing to do is to live in the present moment to the fullest, and remain attached to the thought that the Nature does not know *'harm or hurt'*. It was this culture that gave me courage and comfort to remain in Zambia for so long, whilst so many others lived in a constant state of fear of being robbed and harmed; indeed that is what they attracted to themselves. The eternal law of attraction is *'all of one's concentrated and lasting desires, and thoughts, and therefore also fears, will manifest themselves'*. There is no escape from this, and if there is no escape from this law of attraction, why not live in a state of eternal optimism and gratitude and attract what we desire most?

I was put to the test of my belief by this first experience on return to England. It gave me the courage and wisdom to walk away from what happened, and inspired me to make a clean start again, a much wiser, bigger and stronger person.

Simple as it may sound, it would be an incomplete record though of all that happened to me. The loss of a substantial part of my savings and betrayal of faith did have a traumatic effect on me but fortunately it was short-lived. For a while I thought all was lost and life was not worth living.

What made it worse was what my wife was going through. It became apparent one Saturday morning when I asked her if she was on duty that morning at the nursing home where she had returned to work. Her curt reply was, *"What are we going to eat if I don't go to work?"*

This caused more emotional pain. It was not as if I was on the brink of bankruptcy. There was enough provision to pay for my sons' university education and meet living expenses for a few months but she believed 'all was lost'. The weeks that ensued were the saddest time of my life. But things always work out. As I dwelled on my inner state, realisation came that I could set aside my emotions and learn to live with them. Setting them aside made them smaller by the day. This created room for optimism.

This is exactly what my mother did in 1957 when she became a widow at a young age with six children. She did not wallow in the story of her misfortune and buckle under the strain of being stranded with virtually no means of survival. She took her thoughts away from my father's death and placed them on our lives. Whatever you place your thoughts on will grow. And sure enough we all grew and prospered. Thinking about how she succeeded in life was, and will always be, most inspiring.

I don't like bananas because they increase the level of potassium in my body. I have ignored bananas on the dining table at home for days and seen them shrivel up ready to be consigned to the bin. In the same manner when painful emotions are set aside they wither away until the space created ushers in new feelings of fresh optimism.

In retrospect I can now emphatically say that to fight unhappiness one should first accept it and learn to live with it. Unhappiness grows if one lives within it by making it his or her lasting story. The beginning of the end of my sad story was when I chose to live with my setback. I have known many individuals who spend years seeking sympathy and lamenting to others about the misfortune that has befallen them. This sympathy of others becomes the fuel for their clammy spirit and so their wretched story continues to thrive.

Africa has always been referred to as a jungle by many cynics. When I returned to England, some relations and close family friends teased me as a returnee from a jungle who needed to be taught the ways of the civilised world. I found that rather distasteful, especially in the light of my very first experience with those two gentlemen.

As I grew accustomed to my new environment, I sensed self-centredness and insensitivity on the part of many people I met. The traditional warmth was absent. Everyone appeared to be in a hurry. Time was short and scarce for everyone. There were more cars on the road than I knew back in the seventies. Children had to be driven to and from school because parents feared for their safety. I could not believe there was such a thing as 'road rage' which would cause a driver to come out of the car and assault a road user, in some cases fatally, for lack of driving courtesy, or for causing a minor driving infringement. The customary thank-yous and common courtesies in public places could not be taken for granted amongst the younger generation. A checkout clerk in a store did not see it necessary to make eye contact with the customer and smile. There was a distinct absence of training, except in larger establishments, and the educational levels in most positions appeared to have declined.

One heard, and read, about numerous cases of indiscipline at school. Pupils bullying pupils had regressed to pupils bullying teachers. Bullying had moved from simple threats and harassment to serious bodily harm and even murder of pupils. The presence of unruly pupils had made many teachers become indifferent towards them. Going to school was not a pleasant prospect for many pupils and teachers. Quite aptly someone quipped once that a father knocked on his son's bedroom door, and asked him to come out of bed. The son refused, giving three reasons for not wanting to go to school, *"I hate school, it's boring and kids tease me,"* whereupon the father replied, *"I give you three reasons why you must go; first, it is your duty, second, you are forty-five and third, you are the headmaster!"*

One aspect of the new ministerial or political philosophy of managing the education system that I could not, and have not, come to terms with, is the rating of schools and public declaration of the rankings in some kind of league table. I found official public condemnation of schools as poor performers to be a ruthless and an irresponsible act which can only be highly demoralising for its staff, pupils and their parents. How would an employer view my son's application for a job if he was educated at such a school? Why should my child suffer just because the authorities did not do their job? Would my son forgive me for sending him to such a school?

'If a school does not meet the set criteria, the critical thing to do is to immediately address the deficiencies through training and augmentation of resources, investment in facilities and enforcement of discipline. Publishing rankings and condemning lowly-rated schools is only a reflection on the administration, teachers and parents. It does not lead to a

solution, but rather, in the long run, to a divided society of blame culture. This can also lead to a subtle kind of corruption in the system for judging performance of pupils', I said to myself.

Schools are not commercially run businesses, nor are they like football teams that they have to be slotted in some kind of league table, so the top ones can be celebrated and honoured. Pupils are not production units, and must not, under any circumstance, be treated as defective rejects. Schools are trusted to carry through a curriculum to teach skills, give knowledge and build character. It is no wonder there is an increasing number of faith schools in Britain now. It is a symptom of failing policies. What kind of citizen and leadership is the system producing for the years to come? In the light of the forecast that by the year 2020 India will have 40 million graduates surplus to her requirements, what repercussions does this have for the so called developed countries where education standards are declining?

In the course of writing this book, I referred to a diary note I had written during my few initial months of return to England. Here is what I wrote then, and to my amazement I find no change now, more than a decade later: *'In many families, and certainly amongst several Asian families, egotistic parents' desire for social prestige in many* instances is taking precedence over children's preference or aptitude for a particular academic qualification or craft, thus causing strained relationships between parents and children. On the other hand the modern day youth has unbridled ambitions, craves popularity, dreams of becoming famous and wants to make a lot of money because that is how success is defined. Parents are an obstruction, and are only necessary as the holders of purse strings. Their sense of success is based on comparison with others, and as long as one is ostensibly doing better than all other people in the social and friend circles and receives approval of others, there is a feeling of success. One is tenuously at the mercy of the transitory and ephemeral opinions of others for one''s sense of well-being. There is no care that this can change overnight and destroy one's self image. True success should be measured by how good one feels about oneself perpetually, absence of guilt, what difference one is making to the lives of others and the legacy one is leaving behind. It should have no bearing on one's accumulations, qualifications, credentials, and status, rank and popularity in the community or at work.

Making heaps of money has become a purpose in life for many, instead of a goal. Purpose is eternal and flows in one's consciousness and is embedded in character, whilst goal is finite by value and time. When making money becomes a purpose, it robs one of the softer, emotional human aspects and turns such a person into a perpetual ruthless machine, caring less for people and more for profit, less for character and more for competence, remembering favours given and forgetting loyalties received, exerting more power and less persuasion, exploiting skills of others rather than extolling human virtues, capacities and talents, and knowing the price of everything, but value of nothing. When the passion to be in a business to serve a community or an economic process turns into lust for money, power and reputation, friends and family become less important, children and dependents are materially cared for, but they experience a void within and struggle to create meaning in life. Alienated youth fill the void in their lives by abusing substances and experimenting with drugs, alcohol and sex.

Cases of drug and alcohol abuse amongst the youth, including Asian youth, have become commonplace and a matter of great concern to their parents. One other shocking piece of statistic worth noting is that more than half the number of youth suffer from a nervous breakdown at some point in time before they are thirty years old; alienation, breakdown of relationship, loss of employment, low self-esteem, lack of purpose in life and fear of failure or criticism, being the chief causes.

One fad which is causing immense self-esteem and personality problems, and very often nervous depression amongst teenage girls is the desire to be slimmer. There appears to be a misguided belief that looks matter more than personality, character and talent. Eating creates a deep sense of *guilt, and consequently they eat less to the point of depriving themselves of nutritional elements essential for balanced growth. Lack of balanced growth means the body, mind and soul are out of synchrony. Expression of thought lacks depth and energy.*

There is too much tension and stress. Everyone appears to be on a proverbial treadmill - toiling hard, but not going anywhere. All the basic material needs are more than satisfied, but inner happiness is lacking due to an unexplainable void within. It does not seem to matter so much that they all own houses, cars, several niceties of life and have investments to last a lifetime. For many of them life is without purpose. They are searching for happiness thinking that it is out there somewhere, not realising it is within themselves, and can be experienced upon lessening the load on their minds of the clutter of false thinking, values and perceptions of social environment.'

In a nutshell I sensed a fragmented world with a distinct absence of serenity – a culture glorifying unbridled ambition and material achievement for self. All of this was more than a mild shock to my system, and I wondered whether I had returned from a jungle, or into a jungle. For nearly two decades I had been accustomed to a different social system.

Once, whilst in Zambia, an inquisitive Indian

expatriate asked me why I had left the cosy life in England and come to Africa again. He enquired, *"How is working here different to working in England?"* I thought for a while and my honest reply to him was, *"In England I was working to better my and my family's life. In Zambia I am working to better the lives of others."* It was this sense of purpose to what I was doing that gave me genuine satisfaction, and thus an inner sense of success.

I sensed a kind of void in the society surrounding me. At first I felt badly out of place, *'How can a social environment change so much in less than twenty years?'* was my question to myself. This was not the Britain I knew in the sixties and the seventies. But then I was only in my twenties at that time. I needed help to understand and accept the new climate. Taking heed from Epictetus, a Roman slave who became a distinguished philosopher, *"Men are disturbed not by the things that happen, but by their opinion of the things that happen,"* I was not going to be hung up on rigid opinions – an open mind was required.

At a spiritual level one first of all learns to accept a situation for what it is. The timeless Christian prayer, *'Lord give me the strength to accept things I cannot change, the courage to change things that I can, and the wisdom to know the difference'* was the most appropriate prompt for me in the circumstances, and what I could change were my perceptions.

I came to a conclusion that with fortitude I could survive and succeed in this new climate. The knowing that when I connect to the Nature, it becomes my perfect ally was once again affirmed.

Connecting to Nature to me means letting go of all the clutter I am carrying in my mind that is causing worry, stress, emotional pain and anguish, all borne out of ego. I remind myself that in reality all this is of no consequence to me. When I do this my ego shrivels, which creates room for the spirit to flow and with it flow solutions to all my problems, if indeed they are problems. The modern day socio-economic climate has made it imperative for everyone to realise that there is an acute need for all of us to learn to let go. Those who have not realised this are living in a dense world of only physical form which is riddled with eternal need and a consequent deep sense of failure, frustration and very low self-esteem.

Sadly this is also true of a growing number of young people in Britain of today. Lack of love and recognition from parents, relatives, teachers and the society in general could be resulting in alienating the youth. There is in them a hoard of physical and emotional energy. This is dissipated in all kinds of purposeless activities which after a while become boring and so these teenagers engineer more adventurous and daring undertakings like brutal fights of serious criminal proportions, stealing cars to go on joyrides, unlawful damage to property, drinking alcohol to excess, smoking banned substances and promiscuity.

Deep within, such unfortunate individuals feel lack a real purpose or mission in life. They feel estranged from parents, teachers and society. They did not get something they wanted – attention – attention which will often equate to love. As teenagers they are too shy to ask for it, and that is not the done thing according to their peers anyway. They do not know what they should do, but more crucially they do not know what they do not know. Not being conscious of one's own ignorance is a serious setback. They are not aware or do not believe that inside them are all the ready made systems for manifesting their desires. They have never reached that far into their inner realm.

They need to venture into their inner self and learn to freely express their desires to bring meaning to their lives and joy from feeling connected with all around them, learn to still themselves and harness that energy in them to become creative. But how does a young person who does not know otherwise become creative? Creativity comes from being inspired to do something original, to discover a hidden talent, to improve something, to do good, to be devoted to a worthy cause. The very thought processes and social conditioning of a young person need to be addressed. Offering voluntary service to a charity, helping the infirm and the aged, joining a neighbourhood watch, working to protect others from being bullied at school, reading biographies of men and women who have improved lives of others, taking up sport to provide entertainment and such noble activities can go a long way towards giving the youth a real sense of belonging and self-worth.

I had to take an objective view of the new social and economic backdrop. In the two decades that I had been in Zambia, Britain had been transformed into a land of entrepreneurial individuals, and unfortunately, but not altogether unexpectedly, also a breeding ground for 'cowboys'. But then without the cowboys, how would one be able to see an honest, upright and decent businessman? Without ignorance and mediocrity being on parade, how would one truly appreciate the strength of wisdom? Being away in Zambia I had been able to observe the socio-political scene in Britain from a distance.

For her boldness and the manner in which she came to grips with the Tory leadership, Margaret Thatcher drew my admiration. Her forthright expression of contempt for the existing order and prescription for change, revealed something of a non-conformist in her upbringing. It was her non-conformism that drew me to her. Under her Conservative government, the British economic system received a major transformation. She initiated a programme of radical and bold reforms which have dramatically changed the British way of life and social behaviour for ever.

In the course of the first few years in office she was instrumental in bringing about reform of the trade unions, privatisation of the utilities which had been in public domain for at least four decades, deregulation through formation of quasi-non-governmental organisations, management of health and education along business criteria and direct tax cuts amongst various other measures. The philosophy of her administration was that with more individual self-reliance and less interference from the Government in matters which private individuals were perfectly capable of dealing with, Britain would be a stronger nation and recover from the malaise that had set in.

As time went by individual enterprise, however, became synonymous with profiteering in many instances, especially in the privatisation of public assets. With inside knowledge, many individuals took advantage of share offers in the newly formed companies and immediately sold them for quick gains. Powerful and enterprising property tycoons purchased numerous state-owned properties below market value from corrupt or incompetent Government officials. This was more a reflection of weakness of character and greed on the part of irresponsible people rather than the very act of privatisation.

She was a very strong personality who had a polarising effect on the society. She brought out strong reactions in people. People loved her or loathed her. Her admirers credit her with rescuing the economy from the stagnation of the seventies, whilst her critics accuse her of dismantling the welfare state and destroying much of the country's manufacturing base. The share of agriculture, fishery, mining and manufacturing in the gross domestic product declined.

The Tory government that she installed in 1979 lasted for just under two decades, at the end of which the country had grown tired of seeing more and more opportunism on the part of politicians and less concern for the welfare of the nation. Nearly two generations had gone through the education system under this regime and had now become part of the nation's future leadership and wealth creators. Seeing the new culture at work gave me a momentary sense of despondency, which was conceivable for me at that time in the light of my tragic business investment failure, and visibly no prospect of a comfortable future for me and my family.

Thinking amongst many people in their teens, twenties and thirties was different to what it was when I was that age. The thinking had hardened so to speak. There was far too much self-centredness and shallowness. It was as if some steps in their education and upbringing had been skipped. Many appeared to have grown up far too quickly, as if they had been on some kind of high-breed programme. Subjects at schools and colleges were studied with expediency in mind to pass examinations, essays and theses were written with greater emphasis on meeting the requirement for the number of words rather than the actual substance, and generally it appeared as though there was too much hurry to reap rewards.

What truly saddened me was that there was no room in this environment for anything like J. Krishnamurti's ethos on education which emphasised the real purpose of education as *'not to prepare us for getting a job, but to help us understand the whole process of life'. According to him '...education is about how to love, how to live simply, how to free our minds from prejudice, superstition and fear If the mind does not penetrate beyond its own barriers, there is misery.'* This kind of philosophy would appear to be alien to the modern day educationist. Equally alien, I am sure, would be what Abraham Lincoln had said on character building in his letter to the headmaster of his son's school.

Here is the letter.

"He will have to learn, I know, that all men are not just, all men are not true. But teach him also, that for every scoundrel there is a hero; that for every selfish politician there is a dedicated hero. Teach him that for every enemy, there is a friend. It will take time, I know, but teach him, if you can, that a dollar earned is of far more value than five found… Teach him to learn to lose and also to enjoy winning. Steer him away from envy, if you can. Teach him the secret of quiet laughter. Let him learn early that the bullies are the easiest to lick. Teach him, if you can, the wonder of books, but also give him quiet time to ponder over the eternal mystery of birds in the sky, bees in the sun and flowers on green hillsides.

In school teach him, it is far more honourable to fail than to cheat. Teach him to have faith in his own ideas, even if everyone tells him they are wrong. Teach him to be gentle with gentle people and tough with tough. Try to give my son the strength not to follow the crowd when everyone is getting on the band wagon. Teach him to listen to all men, but teach him also to filter all he hears on a screen of truth and take only good that comes through.

Teach him, if you can, how to laugh when he is sad. Teach him there is no shame in tears. Teach him to scoff at cynics and to beware of too much sweetness. Teach him to sell his brawn and brain to the highest bidder, but never to put a price tag on his heart and soul. Teach him to close his ears to the howling mob and to stand and fight if he thinks he is right.

Treat him gently, but do not cuddle him, because only the test of fire makes fine steel. Let him have the courage to be impatient, let him have the patience to be brave. Teach him always to have sublime faith in himself, because then he will have sublime faith in mankind.

This is a big order, see what you can do. He is such a fine little fellow, my son."

The current system places far more emphasis on teaching subjects like maths and science and to conform to the societal norms and standards rather than educating children and character building. Thus no avenues are created to ask the big questions about life at a young age or to follow one's inner calling. You either fall in line or deviate and be branded a troublemaker.

Matters of heart and soul are secondary to matters of brawn and brain. *Knowledge without character* is one of Gandhi's seven deadly sins which he said will destroy our civilisation. Knowledge without strong principled character is worse than little knowledge.

Winning the race generally seems to be more important than actually running it. Nobody appears to care for losers. Over the years of my life, I have had very many successes in the academic world as well as on sports fields, but on reflection I have found that after every success, be it passing an examination with distinction or winning a sports accolade, there was an anti-climax, a kind of vacuum inside me and a loss of immediate purpose and certainly no discernible joy. The real joy, I am certain, was in the process of studying for an examination or training for a major sporting event, and any minor setback gave birth to a stronger purpose to succeed next time.

The application of various methods of manipulation appears to be justified in all walks of life with little care for mores. Teachers and schools are apparently judged by the number of pupils passing at good grades. Teaching has become more target-oriented as in a commercial business, and the true purpose of teaching is marginalised by the need to remain within financial budgetary allocations. Doing the thing right is more important than doing the right thing.

Profiteering at the expense of the gullible public is so endemic amongst a number of business enterprises and institutions that it is almost regarded by many as ethically acceptable. Distortion and misstatement of facts and broadcasting distasteful and odious programming to glamorise television for ratings gains has become a new culture.

Life appears to be all about being in a competition; many young people fail to realise that competition is only necessary when all are racing for one prize, and if everyone tried to be unique in their own way, competition would become irrelevant. All actions are a strife to bring comfort to one's own life, but the sense of strife for the comfort of another does not feature in most minds. So if there is one chair and two takers of it, the two will compete to decide who will sit on it, not who will stand.

There appears to be a great deal of warped thinking. I think if everyone starts to espouse it, life may become torrid. And this kind of thinking has been on open display on the radio and television, fully justified on the grounds of freedom of expression and one's right to have an opinion and participate in a public debate.

A radio presenter, whilst talking to an investing banker on the subject of massive bonuses for some of the bank's employees, asked him if it was fair to pay such huge bonuses when the teachers were so poorly paid. The reply was, *"If you are making a lot of money for your employer, you deserve to be paid a large bonus. Teachers do not make any money for their employer. Why should they expect more than what they are getting?"* Momentarily the respondent had a memory lapse – he had been a beneficiary of the education system. Or had he? Was he not a product of the education system that put him there? Or was he a victim of an under-funded system?

I believe his reply should have been guided by a thought process that says, *"A banker merely makes money for his employer, but a teacher creates a country's wealth and should be recognised and rewarded accordingly."* The falling birth rate means fewer children, and therefore better opportunities to finance the education of children who are becoming more precious to our well-being.

During a radio discussion on the environment a caller said, *"Why should I care about what is going to happen to the Earth in 100 to 200 years? I want to enjoy myself now."* Yet the same person is enjoying fruits from trees planted long ago by someone who never aspired to eat from them.

During another discussion on devolution and the separation of England, Scotland and Wales, a caller said, *"I have two leeches on my shoulders – one for Scotland and one for Wales."* And in another programme, celebrating a victory at Wimbledon by a Scottish player, one caller said *"No self-respecting Englishman will support Andy Murray. He is Scottish."*

Individuals who are accustomed to dividing and drawing lines between communities will always find differences between people and hence reasons for justifying their petty prejudices. Even if England were a distinct nation, such individuals would probably regard anyone north of Watford as primitive, or call Yorkshire a county of superior people, or fight for independence of Cornwall, depending on exactly where they are based. It is in their nature to split, separate and isolate. They are individualistic rather than universalistic. They exist in a state of constant conflict with the outside world.

"Never trust any of your employees. Keep an eye on each one. The moment you turn attention away from them, they will steal," was the reply from a cash and carry owner when asked about the secret of his success.

In the eyes of such entrepreneurs, employees are no longer viewed as human beings with a sense self-respect and dignity. Why employ people if you cannot trust them? The relationship between an employer and an employee goes beyond the terms of engagement. It is a kind of social contract for the mutual benefit of both parties. A successful businessman is only successful because his employees choose to work for him and devote nearly seventy percent of their waking time to work at his place. This is a significant proportion of one's life for which due recognition, respect, gratitude and reward from the employer would go a long way towards creating a healthy working environment in which all can prosper.

In another instance, a leading businessman said on a popular television programme that he would not like to recruit a business executive who is likely to allow personal emotional problems to affect decisions at work – *"personal domestic matters must be kept away from office"*.

Such culture fails to recognise that employees are human beings – parents and spouses just like their employers. This culture creates a stressful environment in which supposedly successful young executives burn out quickly or suffer serious social setbacks in the interest of their career. Such individuals end up being divorced or guilty of neglecting their children. This kind of culture fails to recognise that a human being is one whole entity that cannot switch on and off between work and home. Some domestic problems cannot be obliterated from the mind and heart upon entering the workplace. A manager who makes sacrifices for the business deserves an understanding employer so that the unwritten partnership between the two can prosper.

In one other instance in a reply to a suggestion that to stop killings amongst school boys, carrying of knives should be made illegal, a teenager said, *"What is wrong with carrying a knife? I need protection. There is no one else to look after me. This is all about looking after number one."*

What is one individual going to do when attacked by a number of youths, all carrying knives? This is a serious indictment on the collective society and its systems if young people feel insecure and, worse still, think that there is no-one to protect them. Taking knives away from them with the might of the law will not change the underlying malaise. Knives can be replaced with boots reinforced with steel toecaps which can be employed equally lethally.

In the highly acclaimed business television programme, The Apprentice, one participant said to another something along the lines of, *"I don't care about your success. Your success is my failure."* Such a culture is symptomatic of an emerging society of highly selfish, individualistic and shallow thinkers playing a zero sum game. Success does not come from defeating anyone but from creating something. This individual forgot that she was there because her mother had succeeded in giving her birth; she was educated because various teachers had succeeded in educating her and she was on that programme because numerous individuals had succeeded in putting the programme together. Success will breed success.

The psychological fragmentation and spiritual void that I discern all around are overwhelming. Faith has been replaced by science and technology. This is a different world – a world of individuals infused with rampant consumerism where self-service takes precedence over self-sacrifice. This is a world of celebrity culture in which people care more for how they look than what they see. Everyone wants to be someone rather than himself first, and is thus living a life of frustration. Wanting to be someone implies dissatisfaction with, and possibly contempt for, oneself. One would rather imitate someone else and wear a fake or borrowed personality to go through life. The idea of changing from within to bring about a self-transformation has no appeal. It is common amongst many people to lay blame on their past and their heritage for their shortcomings.

There is no appeal in being a private citizen and doing low-key public good. Acknowledgement and publicity of one's good deeds are essential prerequisites as just rewards for these deeds. These words of Krishnamurti are an apt reminder of what happens when we want to be someone: *"We all want to be famous people – and the moment we want to be something, we are no longer free... you can be creative only when there is abandonment – which means really when there is no compulsion, no fear of not being, of not gaining, of not arriving."*

Ruthless pursuit of success at work at the expense of others is quite common amongst many young people. In this zero sum game *'scoring goals against others'* is preferred to *'sharing goals with others '*. Prosperity means accumulation, not enriched life. People appear to be rich in material wealth, but poor in time. There is no time for others, hence there is hardly any investment in relationship building. In many instances lack of family ties is destroying relationships and causing excessive violence.

The result, evidently of all this, is emotional insecurity and moral ambiguity.

Thus, on my return to England I saw a world that posed many challenges and equally opportunities for the likes of me to strive towards becoming one in a million, rather than of a million.

On a more pragmatic and positive front, it was a matter of pride that so many East African Asians, and many from Uganda, looked like they had established themselves in all kinds of enterprise, small and large, in retail, manufacturing, distributive and service sectors. Their zeal to progress and industrious nature are evidenced by a plethora of Asian professionals in all fields. Their much-admired work ethic has created opportunities for them to progress in the public as well as the private sectors.

Asians have become much more organised in all walks of life and are beginning to be recognised as an emerging socio-economic class in Britain with a phenomenal spending power that cannot be ignored. Many are listed in the Sunday Times 'Rich List' and it is not unusual to see them amongst the richest.

Seeing the lives of the Asians in a positive light gave me the inspiration to get up and do something. I decided to set up in practice and announced myself as a business analyst and development specialist. That was the kind of work I had done and enjoyed during the previous decade in Zambia. I recalled having worked in collaboration with individuals from international bodies like the World Bank, the IFC, various banking consortia and such multilateral organisations at both micro and macro-economic levels to restructure the Zambian economy. The realisation came to me that I was, and had always been, a very capable professional.

One of the first people I met at a business breakfast cried out during introductions, "Ah, another management consultant!" There was a ring of cynicism in his tone. *"As a lay person I can understand how a holographic representation of a solid object is created by splitting a beam of light, but what a consultant does is an enigma to me. And when I can't figure something out, I stay away from it"*. I did not, and still do not, call myself a consultant, but took the trouble to engage in a lively discussion with him at the end of which I left him with my understanding of the term 'consultant' and what I perceived to be my occupation.

A management consultant is a much derided professional, mainly because such a person cannot be identified with a specific product or service or expertise, and can be supposedly very expensive. Various government departments in the UK, and no doubt many other countries, are notorious at hiring resources from specialist firms to carry out one-off tasks which cannot be handled in-house. Such resources are often wrongly called consultants to the public's chagrin.

A management consultant does not necessarily

solve problems, but rather identifies them and offers solutions. He or she has a knack for a quick grasp of a situation and can analytically examine it to identify bottlenecks, obstacles, impediments or any other drawbacks. The skills for this kind of work are derived from a vast amount of information, applied knowledge, immense experience and intensive training. A consultant examines a given situation from a different and neutral standpoint which lends itself to objectivity and clarity of thought. He or she looks at it from a different window, and helps to bring about a paradigm shift in the way things and situations are viewed. To a large extent a consultant is an educator.

As time passed, I met people from different walks of life and picked up assignments of varying kinds, most of them from recommendations made by family relations, friends and acquaintances. In most of my work I got to know my clients at a personal level. It was important to gain a level of intimacy to find lasting solutions. This gave me insights into their states of consciousness, attitudes to life and people, management styles, personal values and principles, business conflicts and dilemmas and their quality of life.

Difficult though it was, in my work with my clients I tried to refrain from forming any negative judgments about them. If I did not feel comfortable with what they were expecting from me, I simply walked away from them. I did not impose my ideas on them but strived to identify issues of concern and find solutions jointly with them. Most of the assignments were of a specific nature and not repetitive or permanent.

I derived immense satisfaction from leaving lasting positive impressions on my clients, from some of whom I learnt that I had actually been instrumental in bringing about a meaningful change, not only in their organisations, but also in their personal lives. I have personally learnt a great deal about human nature and behaviour and, more specifically, about the unique qualities of those who are successful in business. There are various ways to define successful, but in this instance by 'successful' I mean those few I came to know, socially and professionally, who have amassed material wealth and improved their physical lives having started with humble beginnings under very stressful conditions and adverse circumstances.

These individuals single-mindedly pursue a thought or an idea with clarity, eagerness, passion and joy to manifest their reality. They have no fear of failure or of being criticised or ridiculed. Whilst continuing to fine-tune their constantly flowing desires of what they would like to possess, achieve, know or experience, they exude a high degree of enthusiasm and energy to fulfil their desires, remain patient, but supremely optimistic, about the intended outcome and see no insurmountable storms, potholes or bumps on the way, but only the end result.

I recall one of several notable experiences. A friend of mine, ACP, who would ordinarily be called unschooled by those that are in the habit of classifying people and slotting them in their prejudicial pigeonholes, has built together with his brothers, a thriving electronics business with a number of retail outlets in the heart of London. Never deterred by small setbacks, embarrassments or ridicule from others, he is a powerhouse of courage, determination and faith. These qualities have been foundational to the business success his family can boast today. These qualities are apparent in his social life as well.

One day he invited me to join him for a round of golf with a couple of his business associates at Wentworth in Surrey. On the way I asked him the tee off time whereupon he said, *"it will all be sorted out when we get there."* When I asked if he had actually booked a tee off time, it became clear that he had done no such thing. All he had done was to promise his business associates from abroad that he would treat them to a round of golf at this prestigious club. I became rather apprehensive but was equally curious to know what would happen on arrival at the club. He approached the booking clerk and announced himself and his party of four. There was naturally no booking for us on that day which was fully booked. Somehow, to my utter amazement, he convinced the clerk that there must have been an error on the part of the club, got an apology from him and secured a slot for a four-ball to tee off. This was all done with a routinely relative ease. Later on in the evening he confessed to me that he had made no prior contact with the club. In his simplistic way, he said to me that he just did not believe that without a prior booking it would be impossible to play at Wentworth. All he desired was to treat us all to a round of gold at Wentworth and did not envisage any obstacles.

Seeing themselves as worthy of all they attain, such individuals generally do not see anything as impossible. They thrive on challenging the norms. They have the knack for tuning into and grasping the hidden messages in their psychic environment for inspiration to manifest their reality. Unschooled, unsophisticated or untrained they may be, but they have the knack to actualise their desires.

That is because they have faith in the gift of faculties

bestowed on them by the Nature, particularly intuitive capabilities, and do not see themselves as any lesser than other beings. Their field of knowledge may be narrow, but whatever they know is what they need to know, and they know it in depth to a masterly level which makes them untouchable.

Another striking individual I met socially and now see as a dear friend, popularly known as KD, is a maverick if I ever knew one. This genuinely independent-minded individual, whose thinking and actions I regard as unorthodox, is a fine example of a self-made man, a refugee from Uganda, who has amassed wealth, reputation and a large number of acquaintances and admirers from all walks of life. Now in his seventies, he lives a lavish lifestyle in a wealthy suburb of London. Starting with humble beginnings in business, he may have been classified as unschooled, but KD is a fine example of a man who has learnt from the University of Life what a vast majority of schooled and trained people do not. He has his own beliefs and ways of doing things in business and social life.

Having amassed his wealth from successfully managing a number of his own garages and service stations in London, KD, a deeply religious man, a teetotaller and a vegetarian, who will refrain from gambling, has read numerous books to gain knowledge on self-improvement and practises Pundit Chanakya's ethics in politics and economics. Thinking big, thinking fast and thinking ahead, believing in diarising his thoughts and intentions, he proudly enthuses over his own beliefs and principles for success in business.

Planning, intelligent marketing, promotion and control are his cherished prerequisites for success. His *Eight Ms,* he says, must be possessed by an entrepreneur for success in any business undertaking. These are money (working capital), material (equipment), merchandise (stock), methods (systems and procedures), marketing, manpower, management, all of which are easy to understand, but the eighth one staggers me. This is where the originality of a deep thinking person manifests itself. It is '*mafia technique*'. He explains that it does not mean one behaves like a gangster or a thug or a bully, but one does go about with airs and graces of a successful and powerful man. This is done by being seen at business, social and public events with an air of uniqueness, such as being noticeably dressed, arriving with flourish and fanfare, being accompanied by beautiful ladies or, if necessary, a couple of hugely built bodyguard-like associates. *"This sends a message to all that this man is powerful and serious about having his way - he had better be taken seriously,"* he says. *"Before going into any important meeting, find out all you can by any possible means about the other party, and always go to all meetings showing courage, no matter what odds are stacked up against you. Outwit the other party, but do not make any person look small. To win a deal, make the other person feel big,"* he says with intent and a sparkle in his eyes.

Truly successful individuals possess unique qualities. And they strive to balance all aspects of their lives for the ultimate self-actualisation.

Others who may amass wealth can often become so deeply immersed in the misguided pursuit of their desires that everything else in life becomes secondary, and often the consequence of this is loss of balance between physical, social, psychological and spiritual aspects of life.

Here are some other observations:

Self-made individuals in business do not trust anyone. Their success comes from keeping a sharp eye on all aspects of the business. They like to be in control all the time and are quick to extricate themselves from situations where control is slipping away from them. This characteristic can spill over into their social lives and so they are often in discomfort at social events where someone else appears to be taking control, or gaining ascendancy over them, or receiving more attention from others.

Individuals successful in business who are not regarded as schooled are truly self-made and can have a great deal to offer about simple thinking in business. They drop out of schooling at an early age and learn to fend for themselves. In business they have less time for, and see no value in, things like written business plans, procedures and elaborate presentations, too many business theories and principles, excessive formality and incomprehensible compliance.

They do not trust a written word as much as they trust a person who speaks the simple truth without the use of weasel words. They cannot always explain their decision in an articulate manner, but they know what is good and right for them. They have the knack to see the dimensions that a schooled person is not trained to do. They rely more on what the stomach says rather than any reasoned thinking. They are genuinely loyal and grateful to their long-serving employees and reward them over and above the norms. They have a few simple beliefs about succeeding in business and always go by these. They may be less read, but whatever they have read and understood, they adopt as their basic truth and remain loyal to it.

Wherever money, accumulations and fame are the only bases for measuring success, there is generally a void inside. There are misguided individuals who believe they have made it as soon as there is evidence of wealth in their possession or fame. They have proved that they are no lesser beings than others. Their arrogance takes over their lives and consequently they alienate everyone around them, their employees, associates, neighbours, family, relations and friends alike. A time comes when there is extreme loneliness in this kind of life that is not properly balanced between principles and values. Pleasure derived from material things is short-lived as there is a distinct shortage of love, tolerance, compassion and understanding of genuinely warm-hearted people in their lives. There is more form than feelings in their existence.

Business activities not in the public interest and profit motives are justified on the grounds of a 'business is business' principle and thus conventionally accepted rules of ethics and basic morality are conveniently set aside. Our basic roles in life are inter-related in a holistic ecosystem of existence. Gandhi said, *"One man cannot do right in one department of life whilst he is occupied in doing wrong in any other department. Life is one indivisible whole."*

When there is a split personality between personal

life and public behaviour, it portends possible mental stress or physical ill health because such incongruous conduct is unnatural and in the long run can lead to numerous side effects of persistent guilt-ridden existence.

Greed, jealousy and personal agendas amongst stakeholders stifle further growth of successful businesses. This is pertinent in family-owned businesses as the family becomes larger and the ownership passes, or does not as the case may be, from one generation to another. Children, spouses of children and grandchildren have varying aspirations and bring different influences from outside, thus the culture that founded the business diminishes and strife takes hold.

A socially pleasant and agreeable fellow can be a different creature in business. People succeed in business because they always want to apply their business policies, win and be right. They will entertain a friend lavishly at a social event but profit from the same friend when he comes knocking on the business door. Social friends are not business friends and business friends are not social friends.

Blatant lies in business dealings are justified as an integral part of business culture. Any deliberate misstatements, or manipulations, contrived to profit the business, or its owner, are construed as ingenious commercial machinations without which a firm cannot survive, and if the firm is not stable or progressive it cannot create employment. This is how basic untruths are rationalised to avoid paying taxes, to generate super profits or to defeat competition. Being practised in the interest of the business is what justifies them and makes them clever lies, and not immoral acts.

In business they don't give anything for nothing. Business is not a charity. Every transaction or deal has to yield a positive benefit to the business at some point in time. This applies to even charitable donations which are made from the business to advance the cause of the business. There is no such thing as a favour. Favours are generally deeds done for those who have the potential to reciprocate at appropriate time.

In their fanatical zeal to grow rich, they make people secondary and drop them like hot potatoes when these people have no more to offer. This is a hallmark of many individuals who care less about people around them when these individuals have no more to offer as a means to a goal. There is no regard for any need for growth through training of the very people who stood by them when they were rising. These people are seen as a barrier to goal achievement.

Truly wealthy individuals are very ordinary people. Those who have amassed great wealth through decades and generations of hard work and application tend to be falsely regarded by others as being in a superior class. These individuals themselves have no sense of superiority or arrogance about them. They are more at home in the company of very ordinary friends doing very ordinary things socially. Without these friends they are very lonely. KRP is one extraordinary entrepreneur in the hotels business I have known as a friend as well as a relative through marriage of a nephew. He exemplifies the virtues of a truly wealthy individual who will, at the risk of appearing to be flaunting his wealth, strive to do ordinary things in the most extraordinary style to show that he cares for his family, relatives, friends and business associates, and yet behind the display of splendour there is an unassuming and kindly man who wants to be in the company of and share his joy and success with others. A devout Hindu who invites a number of guests to his home at religious ceremonies every year and follows direction of his spiritual guide, he displays no arrogance or air of superiority.

I tracked down and renewed acquaintance with many of my old friends from back home in Uganda. I could not believe how warm and receptive they were towards me. As we reminisced on our younger days, it amazed me how many fond memories of me they had treasured. They were full of complimentary and encouraging remarks.

I recall running into an old classmate in a restaurant in California. He was with his family, and in the midst of our joyous recollections, he turned to his teenage sons and said, *"If you can be half as good as uncle Anil was at school, I will be a very happy father!"* The deep respect my friends had for me came to the surface. I cannot think of better self-worth restoring words.

That's not all. In another instance, a childhood friend of mine, MGG, with whom I share many joyous moments, and now also work, once after he, his wife Shila and I had had a dinner at a restaurant, narrated to her an incident that astounded me. The incident had taken place at a cricket match in our hometown, Mbale, in Uganda. He said to her something like, *"The most memorable incident on a cricket pitch I recall from about forty years ago was when a very prominent Ugandan opening batsman called Nurdin was run out by a brilliant piece of fielding from Anil in the first over of a national league match. Nurdin could not believe that such a young player could have the presence of mind and such a strong arm as to hurl the ball and hit the wicket, from about thirty five yards away, so accurately and so fast as to catch him out of his crease and run him out".*

I could not believe that anybody would have remembered and recalled that incident so vividly; I did not even know that MGG was present at that match, but he had savoured that incident about which I had never made a mention to anyone thinking it would be of little interest to others. This is a great strength of his – the capability to lucidly recall the past from which he has drawn many a lesson. Although he is a professionally qualified accountant, he has made his fortune from building a successful and highly reputable travel insurance brokerage. And yet he regularly recalls his humble beginnings and what valuable lessons he has learnt from numerous individuals on his way to prominence in the UK travel insurance industry.

In spite of his success, he still seeks the warm comfort of the company of his old friends who may not have attained his status in life. He does not pretend to have forgotten where he has come from, nor where he belongs.

The basic essence of a truly successful person does not change with circumstances. MGG often relives the experience of how his family had to suffer humiliation in the aftermath of his father's business setback, and lives by his vow never to be at the mercy of any creditor – he cherishes the virtue of living within one's own means. He has sterling attributes which are foundational to his accomplishments in all walks of life. Thinking big with graphic imagination and being strong-willed, he applies his business and organisational skills with extraordinary zest. His keen eye for detail and commercial deal-making handiness are his notable traits.

Apart from being shrewd and industrious, he is a voracious reader who constantly craves information and ideas to bring innovation and strength to his business. The strong will follows strong desire to accomplish and not only does he not shun from performing disagreeable and unsavoury tasks, but actually makes it his purpose to attack them with verve and carries the countenance of confident expectation for positive outcomes. He is a mental giant.

H Ray is another school-boy friend whom I tracked down in the USA after a gap of some thirty years. He is not someone I would have called an academic giant at school, but he has been highly inspirational to me in writing this book and I say without hesitation that he is a scholar from the University of Life.

At school it was evident that his mind was not in

pursuit of further education. He had a burning desire to be his own master and succeed in business. Not averse to taking risks and fearless in the face of any and all challenges, he found himself with his family in Canada like many exiles from Uganda. Not finding any business opportunities totally to his liking, he set off for the USA with his brother in search of fortune.

Having driven long distances for days and feeling extremely low in spirit they came to stay for a night in a run-down motel in a remote town in New Mexico. This stay turned out to be a signature moment in his life. The state of the motel stirred the inquisitiveness of an enterprising mind in him. Further enquiries revealed that the owner was interested in selling. Seeing the potential to turn the business around by improving the property and being offered vendor finance, they found themselves owning a motel within a few days. That is how he made a start to his meteoric success in business.

In less than two decades H Ray was a proud owner in his own right of a number a high-class motel franchises and commercial and residential properties in the USA and Canada. This dream-fulfilling success has come not only from just hard graft, but also from learning and applying the necessary technical and managerial skills, and self reliance.

However, his biggest attribute is his positive 'I can and I will' mental attitude complementing a strong desire to attract to him like a magnet not only material success, but also knowledge about life and enlightenment. He reads inspirational works of renowned authors and has been able to balance the physical, social, psychological and spiritual aspects of his life.

Such are my millionaire friends. I have been very proud of them and have learnt to experience joy whenever I think of their good fortune. Feeling joy for them puts my consciousness in harmony with theirs. I am then welcomed into their world to enjoy the privilege of their hospitality.

However, notwithstanding all that internal, emotional, impalpable stuff, at one stage when I must have gone into a depressive state, I found myself thinking that '*my family must be harbouring thoughts that all my friends have made it, and I have got nowhere. What good are my professional qualification, extensive experiences, sporting achievements and all these friends if I have to toil hard and can't have all the luxuries they enjoy?*'

I found myself to be quite sombre for a few weeks, not able to shake off these thoughts from my mind. I began to think I was a failure in life. Not only that, I began to think my entire life up to this point had been founded on wrong kind of thinking and unworkable beliefs. *I should have been striving to be like them, full of fight and hyper-competitive in the fast lane,* I thought to myself. In reality I had not emerged from my failed business venture or the shock of being deceived. Deep down I was in despair and in need of guidance. Was I viewing life with a jaundiced eye?

ELEVEN

TOWARDS FLAWLESS VISION

"If I have a conclusion about you, which is an opinion, a judgement, an evaluation, an image about you, I am obviously not related to you"

J. Krishnamurti

What BR had introduced me to in Zambia, stood by me. Seeking an oasis of tranquillity amidst violent tides of change and hankering after guidance and some answers, I found walks in the evening most inspiring. I sought and thrived more and more on solitude which became a perfect catalyst for much needed introspection. I began to look for quiet moments to observe silence and reflect on events.

I found, for the first time in my life, that these moments of silence, not loneliness I might add, were most inspiring, enlightening, invigorating, and thus therapeutic. I started to experience bouts of total absence from thought when I sat comfortably, in contemplation, and with closed eyes, allowing my mind to flow freely. This exercise would last between five and fifteen minutes at the end of which I would have no recollection of any kind. It was akin to self-induced suspended animation, or momentary stillness of time, or erasure of a part of my immediate past. Opening my eyes at the end of the experience was not like waking from normal sleep, nor was it like regaining consciousness from being anaesthetised. I would feel energised and renewed. It was as if I had shut down and let in the force of Nature to do its work without interference from my ego; like shutting down and handing over a manufacturing plant to engineers for routine maintenance so that all the machinery is restored to optimal working order.

This is now a routine I follow a number of times every week for a set number of minutes. It finishes at near enough the predetermined time, sometimes uncannily almost to the minute. It enables me to empty my mind of any obstacles like fear and anxiety. As a result, I am at ease with myself and emotionally free, meaning not free of emotions but instead, not slavishly attached to any idea or object and yet still sensing a kind of connectedness with all and everything. I say without any hesitation that these esoteric experiences in the inner are sporadic, though I make no claim to being an adept at this skill.

As days turned into weeks, my strengths and faculties began to come to the surface. Thus began the process of getting to know my true self. After a short self-re-evaluation period, it dawned on me that my rather jaundiced, gloomy and negative observations of the new environment were merely a result of flawed interpretation of the information my mind had processed, and nothing else. These judgements were based on my point of view, which others did not have to agree with. I was comparing life then with life I knew in my younger days, and the life I knew again in Africa.

Not everyone saw my second-time life in Britain from my perspective. I had not yet surfaced from the cesspit of comparing and judging. I realised the folly of expressing any judgement, cynicism, or even having any desire to do so. It dawned on me that to express a strong hateful opinion and ridicule, or to condemn, or show indifference was no different to employing malicious propaganda or a weapon as destructive and lethal as a loaded gun. '*Deep seated and strong hateful emotions reach their target via the inner path and invite matching responses. At the highest level such an attitude breeds a culture of recrimination and counter-recrimination, which polarises societies into hostile groups filled with mistrust of one another'* was what the voice inside me had to say.

I felt that as long as I was looking for someone to blame for anything that I misperceived as having gone wrong in my world, or I was filled with any anger, contempt, condemnation or indifference, I was a walking, talking, living, human bazooka programmed to wreak devastation. The vibrations I was emitting were not healthy for my social surrounding.

I am now of firm belief that this kind of contemptuous attitude, indifference and ridicule towards others, when prevailing widely, leads to fragmentation of a nation, or lack of harmony in societies. If any young and underprivileged people are subjected to such attitude, they soon become disaffected and, not surprisingly, indulge in excessive drinking, crime and violence as a natural consequence. Similarly if ethnic groups, or social classes, are seen as distinctly characterised by their culture and language, they remain so and become stronger as that in a polarised environment.

I drew a positive from my superficial observations of the social environment when I looked at it as a set of circumstances orchestrated for me by the Higher

Intelligence with a purpose. There was nothing to be gained from being pessimistic or despondent about my early observations, other than to give reins to debilitating forces. These were my observations which did not necessarily portray truth from another person's standpoint.

If they were true, they merely represented my truth at that time. They were giving me a measure of myself in the world of relativity and enhancing my sense of awareness, in the same way as you, the reader of this book, are deriving a measure of yourself at this present moment.

It was crucial for me to cease to feel unconnected and different from others, and to forgive and start to love myself as a worthy being who had come to a realisation that he had a great deal more to know about himself.

You always find what you are looking for.

I expressed a desire to feel a sense of connectedness with others and to explore what was lurking inside me that was preventing me from opening up. I came to realise it was fear, fear of failing again. But at the highest level there is no such thing as a failure; failure is just an experience that changes behaviour. There is no stigma to it. It is a part of living.

Life is in a state of flux; a constant change. It is its primary characteristic. I change by the minute, my body changes every second, seasons come and go and everything I see around me on this planet is changing. So what is strange about my observations of my environment? The change just is. It is here to stay.

Change is the only permanent characteristic of life. It is the very spice of life. There is no need to express any opinion about it other than to know that because life is changing, it is wise to live every moment to the fullest. The wise who live free from the baggage of their past and perceive the future as the next present moment, are worthy of eternal joyful life. They are eternally vibrant and never feel immobilised.

By using my faculties and talents, I gain knowledge about my environment which adds to all the accumulated content only to boost my ego, but I don't know the environment. The knowing can only come when I become totally infused in it, just like a grain of salt in water. To do so, I have to reach out, open up to my surrounding and accept it for what it is without qualifying it. Only then can I begin to truly understand and influence it. Salt will only change the taste of water when it dissolves in it.

When I internalised this thought process, I

experienced a paradigm shift and wonderful feelings started to make a home in my heart. All of a sudden everything was right with life in essence. There was no need to be hung up about anything as I am responsible for creating my circumstances through choices I have exercised. There is no such thing as bad weather when I choose to make it myself. I just had to get on with life without the need to be pessimistic about anything because I don't know what is lurking round the corner, waiting to happen. It could be something unimaginably wonderful.

My consciousness was discernibly growing. I began to intuit the hidden dimension. Life is a perpetual drama with a purpose. Yesterday's truth has become a lie today, and today's truth will become a lie tomorrow. Slavery is no longer tolerated in almost every part of the world. Homosexuality is now accepted as normal. No-one in their right mind will call Nelson Mandela a terrorist even though he spent decades in jail under that charge. A pupil branded at school as no good, mediocre and disgracefully discharged for intolerable behaviour can become a successful businessman who also owns schools offering free education to underprivileged children.

Stepping away from rigid stereotypes and the

inclination to deride and condemn, but remaining passionately attuned to the practice of fulfilling living, crafted out of the crucible of daily grind, is the gateway to the world of invisible realities – a shift from knowledge to knowing.

Everything natural, everything physical, every custom, every tradition, every belief, every civilisation goes through the unending process of change, reform, growth, disuse and decay, and every sunrise heralds a renewal and ushers a new beginning. Seasons come and go without fail and without any human intervention. There can be nothing but optimism riding on the underlying eternal unifying force that holds together all that I can see and sense as being in a state of integrity. There is definitely an extraordinarily great force at work that is responsible for the existence of all the wondrous and astounding happenings.

I am only an instrument through which it acts when I open myself to it. The likes of me have come and gone, and more will come and go in an unending procession, but the carrying force will prevail. The words of Carl Jung give as close a fitting representation of my feelings as I can think. *"Life has always seemed to me like a plant that lives on its rhizome. Its true life is invisible, hidden in the rhizome. The part that appears above ground lasts only a single summer. Then it withers away – an ephemeral apparition. When we think of the unending growth and decay of life and civilisation, we cannot escape the impression of absolute nullity. Yet I have never lost a sense of something that lives and endures underneath the eternal flux. What we see is the blossom, which passes. The rhizome remains."*

I now look at, and interpret, the world differently - meaning I am a much more tolerant and resilient individual and my perceptions of life have evolved. I choose to accept events and situations as part of an unending natural cyclical process having been orchestrated for me for a purpose. I strive to draw a positive in every situation because everything happens for the best, and time tells how that is so.

In 1958, in the aftermath of my father's death, my mother decided overnight that she would not be returning to India, to live with relatives, with all six of her children, choosing to remain in Uganda. This may have appeared to be a highly risky and foolish decision at that time, but little did I know then how that choice would change, for the better, the entire course of life for all of us.

When I see now how her six children have grown into a family of thirty-nine with spouses, children and grand-children, amongst whom are accountants, engineers, a dentist, a pharmacist, an optometrist, an audiologist, graduates and businessmen, my belief is reaffirmed that everything happens for the best. This belief is empowering and enabling because, at first, it makes me accept what has happened and then it systematically and responsively goes to work with me in the inner as a guiding force to deliver the desired outcome. I do not bury my head in the sand and feel immobilised.

I feel compelled to share with you a dream experience without the mention of which this chapter cannot be concluded. This dream precedes, and is foundation to, my paradigm shift and the ongoing process of exfoliation of layers of ingrained conditioning. As a result I now know that I am no more a prisoner of warped thinking nor a slave to the illusory social norms and imposed sense of moral right and wrong, without any of it being in total harmony with my inner guiding mechanism. I challenge conventional wisdom and my consciousness refuses to believe in and accept any social norms, unless they make absolute sense to me and do not disconnect me from anyone or anything. I am generally well composed and at total ease with myself because I no longer allow most situations to disconcert me.

In this dream, which even today is as clear to me as daylight, I was sleeping, face down when I heard the clearest and sweetest sound of bells ringing as if in the distance. The sound became louder and louder by the second. I lifted and turned my head towards the bedroom door. The sound of the bells became much sweeter and louder as the door opened to let in a ball of white light. Out of this light emerged a glowing radiant face of a monk. He stood tall in a white robe, looking vibrant and wise, but it was difficult to tell his age for there was a healthy look about him. His lively, creaseless face, that was clean-shaven like his head, bore a wholesome loving smile that revealed a fine set of teeth and his sparkling eyes were resplendent with tender love as he clearly and crisply spoke the words *"It's time to wake up"* and then disappeared. I woke up immediately and looked for him. He was not there. I was all by myself and momentarily felt lonely as I lay in bed, gazing in wonder at the barren bedroom wall in front of me. I noticed that I was breathing hard as if I had been running a marathon race.

I was so moved by this unique experience that for the first few days I could not think of anything else during quiet moments. As I recall, since then there has been an ongoing transformation of my inner self. I see dimensions that I did not think existed or could be sensed or seen. I see no right or wrong, good or evil, moral or immoral acts. There is no real anxiety about anything; there is no stress, no sensitivity to the opinions of others about me. I see clearly the futility of comparing, contrasting and competing in matters of daily living. Religious and racial differences mean less to me now as there is in me a growing sense of affinity with all and everything. I am certain the mysterious monk is visiting millions of people and exhorting them to "wake up".

My waking had begun.

Firstly I became totally detached from the desire to smoke. I used to smoke large cigars – at least two a day - for a number of years. I needed a cigar when I was engaged in intensive work at my desk, I needed a cigar after a meal, I needed a cigar when I was driving, playing golf, walking in the street, whenever and wherever. It was demanded by my ego, it was good for my image and it enhanced my reputation. My friends used to bring me cigars because they knew I loved them. One morning whilst seated at my desk in my study I reached for a Havana, and instinctively uttered to myself '*do I need this?*' as I held it in my hand. '*No!*' was an emphatic answer from inside me. I threw the cigar in the bin, then I took one look at the box of the remaining Havanas on my desk and decided its home was in the bin. Next I stood up and, in some kind of frenzy, grabbed hold of all the boxes of various varieties of cigar in the cupboard and shoved them in the bin. In less than five minutes I disposed of several hundred pounds worth of cigars. I say with no hesitation that is the best investment I have ever made. Since then I have not once had an urge to smoke. My teeth and gums are healthier, my taste buds have come alive so I enjoy eating, my nasal sense has also become sharper and my breathing has improved. I feel clean and younger, and I have not put on any more weight, contrary to common belief.

I often wonder if it was this simple for me to give up smoking, why so many individuals struggle to give it up. My answer is that when I truly link up with my real self, who is the inner self, the conflict between the egoistic personality and the spirit within is resolved. The ego succumbs and the spirit prevails.

In my case it had nothing to do with smoking being right or wrong, good or bad, healthy or unhealthy, gaining others' approval or not and fair or unfair to society, but it had everything to do with truly liberating myself from the clutches of a habit. I was a slave to an evil master residing inside me. But realising that I was the landlord, I brought its tenancy to an end, banished it for ever and thus freed myself. For me to link up with my inner self means to think about my thoughts, actions, desires, emotions and anxieties, and thus generally stay in a heightened sense of self awareness, but remain patient and leave solutions to predicaments and all supposedly insurmountable problems to the force of Nature – it knows when and how to provide answers. This is my way to surrender and express faith.

Giving up alcohol thereafter was simple. I was a renowned whisky drinker although I never overindulged. It only took one brief experience that has left a lasting, but positive, impression on me. One early morning while staying at a hotel, I had to help lift up a young, handsome man, the only son of a very dear friend, and take him to his room. He had been lying face down on the floor in the reception area of the hotel till the early hours of a Sunday morning after bingeing the previous night. As we stumbled towards his room, I saw his acquiescent wife, who had heard all the commotion, standing in the doorway in tears, but feeling apologetic towards me, her tender, youthful face telling me '*I have to live with this everyday*'. I think she felt embarrassed that this shameful side of her married life was now in the open.

I helped seat him on his bed and rushed back to my room, dismayed and distraught. As I sat on my bed, some force overcame me and I burst into tears. I was saddened because I was helpless. I was helpless because I was not myself a fitting model for him. This incident tormented me for several days. It is the likes of me who are responsible for the youth who are misguided into believing that *'alcohol is cool'*. *Was I indifferent and uncaring?* The answer was an emphatic 'yes'.

He needed help, but I was immobilised. I was morally weak and for as long as I continued to partake of alcohol I was of no assistance to anyone who was in the grips of alcohol. I had to become and feel like a worthy mentor. To earn the right to say to someone *'alcohol is no good for you'* and say it with vigour and positive energy, I had to become free of alcohol. And I did. All I had to do was to say to myself that *alcohol was no more a part of my life* and not only mean it, but also feel that I was totally cleansed of alcohol. I have not since missed it. I do not condemn anyone who takes alcohol, but I feel that I am worthy of listening and talking to anyone who wants to gain mastery over alcohol.

When in 1967 I was asked to leave the college, I wanted to change the world so no underprivileged person is denied education. But true education is attained, not by paying fees, but in the experiences of living – in the University of Life. No one can deny anyone this education. The wounds dealt on my psyche needed a process of self-healing, purification and cleansing. I had to strive to free myself from the states of need, anger, judgment and prejudice which are mere illusions that I can live with, but not within, for I have broken and continue to break the shackles of living within.

I believe this freeing has come from a set of self-cultivated and practised principles and belief statements – basic truths so to speak. It has been said, *'as you think, so shall you be.'* Thoughts, riding on the energy of powerful emotions, lead to results. Consistent results from the same continued thoughts result in beliefs. Sustained beliefs result in fundamental truths which become principles over time. Principles become the basis of well reasoned guiding tenets.

I would finally like to share some of my cherished mind- and soul-liberating guiding tenets with you. They are my companions of immense value and transformational wisdom. They serve me well whenever I find myself to be in a quandary, fear-bound, low in spirit, or dwelling too much on negative thoughts. They are an invaluable basis for abandonment and understanding the enduring daily drama we call living.

TWELVE

BARRIER-SHATTERING PRINCIPLES

1

"HONOUR THE SPIRIT IN ALL"

This first principle is based on the understanding that no matter how much an individual may disagree with my beliefs, no matter how vehement we may both be in stressing our point of view, no matter how emotional we may become in asserting our respective views, we cannot allow these differences to stand between us as human beings.

Fundamentally, I believe that there is no such thing as right or wrong. Everything just is. I do not allow someone's ridicule of my opinion or belief to touch my inner-self even when I am met with very personal and derogatory remarks.

I come across individuals who are so hardened in their way of thinking that they ungraciously rebuff a different point of view without even hearing it fully. I do not engage in debate with such individuals and instead choose to hear what they have to say. This approach has the effect of taming the ego which takes all the anger and negative emotions out of a discussion or a spat. But most importantly, it does not make me swerve from the need to honour the spirit in the other person because fundamentally there is no difference or distance between me and them.

Differences of opinion come from a number of causes - deep mistrust, lack of proper knowledge, a basic misunderstanding, misinterpretation, the need to be right or simply to have one's own way. Each person has the right to have point of view, a belief system, a desire to exist in harmony with everyone around him in all circumstances, even when there is an intense disagreement over a point. Each one of us has a spiritual or psychic space around us, and this space forms a cocoon that shields us from being invaded by the harmful thoughts of others. To enter the spiritual space of a person, one's mind has to be vibrating in synchrony with that spiritual space and convey a message of recognition of that person's soul as a sacred entity.

I have learnt that it is possible to strike an accord with anyone in any circumstance providing I recognise that person to have feelings and emotions like me. This is a simple, but sincere, process of expressing this thought silently to myself. When I do this, my body language, the expression in my eyes, my mannerisms, speech and tone send signals to the other person who immediately senses the warmth in me towards him at a deep level and instantly experiences a transformation in his consciousness.

It was in Zambia one morning that I had an unforgettable experience whilst on a long road journey. I had been driving for nearly two hours, and I was far from any urban civilisation, so to speak. I found myself driving through a forest when there was a sudden dip in the road that was filled with a patch of low-lying early morning mist. To my utter horror and rather late I saw in front of me a vehicle being slowly towed by an old pick-up van. I applied the brakes but still a minor collision was unavoidable. The drivers of the two vehicles before me stepped out making wild, impassioned gestures and ranting on about the damage done to their property by my car. Hearing the commotion, several local dwellers gathered and in no time there was a crowd sympathising with the aggrieved drivers of the cars with which my vehicle had struck.

Momentarily I feared the angry crowd would turn

on me. It is a trait amongst many African tribes to attack any driver that causes an accident. I had a vision of finding myself walking on the road barefoot, wounded and stripped of all my belongings. Remaining fully composed and unflappable, I stepped out of my car and started to examine the damage done to the vehicles. The crowd was momentarily silent. The owner of the car then started to protest and demanded to know how I was going to compensate him for the dent in the rear of his car; the crowd expressed agreement with his demand. Some of them stared at me with angry facial expressions.

I still remained composed and assured him that he would receive justice. I was not interested in the least in defending my case even though both the other vehicles were un-roadworthy, untaxed, without a towing permit and there was no reflective sign at the back of the towed vehicle. I gently walked up to the driver of the vehicle being towed and placing my hand on his neck enquired if he was in pain, as I feared he might have suffered a whiplash. There was a look of surprise on his face and then sudden calmness overcame him as he shook his head and said he was not hurt. I offered to take him to hospital. He did not see the need for it and stood there for the next gesture from me. I offered to have his car repaired, but somehow he decided he did not want to pursue the matter further. There was calm and the tension in the crowd melted as I shook hands with two drivers. We proceeded on our ways.

I can only surmise that this astonishing outcome came about from my firstly recognising him as an aggrieved and injured human being without any attempt to apportion any blame on him, whilst remaining calm and considerate.

In a similar context I know a story of a woman whose husband said to her, *"I have invited our bank manager for dinner tonight. He and I are going to finalise our business loan deal"*. She undertook to put on a fitting dinner.

Later that afternoon she drove to the supermarket to buy provisions, but coming back she was held up in the traffic and the preparation was bound to be delayed. As soon as she was out of the busy road, she drove off fast. In trying to reach home quickly, she skipped a red traffic light and collided with another vehicle crossing her path at the junction. Coming out of her car and seeing that there were no potential witnesses in sight, immediately accused the other driver of careless driving in an outpour of angry words.

The other driver calmly proposed to call the police and allow them to decide on the matter. After the police had taken statements from both the parties, she drove home in her car which was not so badly damaged, but the other vehicle had to be towed away. Later that evening, the bank manager arrived in a taxi. She rushed to answer the door. As he introduced himself, she froze in the doorway.

She could not believe that he was the very man in the car that she had collided with and angrily accused of careless driving. He noticed how mortified she was at the sight of him and so pretended not to recognise her. That way his hostess was able to come out of her predicament to entertain him and enjoy the rest of the evening. He chose not to hurt her spirit for his own ego's sake. The matter of the loan for her husband's business was far more important to her than his own desire to humiliate her. He honoured the spirit in her and in the process both of them experienced an ineffable sense of relief. A few years later her husband became one of the bank's most important clients.

In the normal course of daily life I come across all kinds of situations with the people I interact with. They can be colleagues at work, clients, customers, neighbour, motorists on the road or a total stranger in the street. My greatest joy comes when each person has shown a kind of warm regard for me and willingness to accommodate me and my needs. My self-esteem receives a boost when I am made to feel that I matter and my opinion is important.

Deepest sorrow comes from a conflict or a strong disagreement with others on a point of principle. This state of being is weakening and uninspiring. It can have serious repercussions for my state of physical, psychological and spiritual health. This is when my integrity begins to wane and I become a lesser person disconnected from others.

Integrity is what holds together, not only nations, but the entire cosmos. Integrity is the bedrock of the universe. Without integrity, it would collapse and cease to be. It has been said that the basic characteristics of the universe are extended in all of us. We are of the universe.

Every cell in a human body, whilst performing its unique function, is connected with all the multitude of cells which constitute a human body. There is a connective force that holds them together, which is present in and around all of us. We are all in the same soup. It is apparent that at the highest level we are all one entity endowed with the same qualities and mysterious enabling power. It is this power which makes it possible to tune into the universal mind that is the source of all inspiration and creative imagination. The super intelligent Force has localised its aspects in each one of us to maintain that connectedness.

So at the deepest level we are in that Force and that Force is in us. We are one with it! This very basic understanding is fundamental to a peaceful, blissful and rewarding existence. It enables me to reach out, and when I do that, I trigger a healing force.

I feel I am awake and truly and eternally alive when I honour the spirit in all.

2

'RUN YOUR OWN RACE'

When life has been lived to its fullest extent there are no regrets in the old age. There are no unfulfilled lifelong desires or shattered dreams, there are no unsung songs rearing to explode, or stifled fantasies, or undeclared love simply because circumstances and other dictates of life did not let them sprout.

Each one of us is endowed with an independent will that is an enabling mechanism for us to shape our lives and become what befits our innermost spark. A controlled exercise of will, which makes things happen in accord with one's inner voice, is a hallmark of a proactive person. Such a person lives by his or her own desires and takes total responsibility for the outcome. Proactive individuals are not scripted by others, nor do they surrender to the will of others. They strive to be unique in everything they do, and are not easily influenced or swayed from their purpose. Their strength and courage are visible in their non-conformity with established practices. They have the courage of their conviction, and are not afraid of the consequences of their actions. They believe that ultimately their will has to prevail. They do not have a herd instinct, and are not ashamed to be seen to be marching out of step with all the rest, for they are listening to the beat of their own drummer. They seek to be *'one in a million, rather than one of a million'*. They strive and make it their endeavour to live their purpose.

This principle demands total faith in oneself, patience to await the desired outcome, courage to withstand ridicule and criticism and exercise of restraint from being swayed to go along with the popular norms.

Such individuals do not seek to measure themselves by reference to others or by their accumulations, identity, qualifications, titles or any such transient attributes. They are not in competition with anyone nor do they seek to gain any kind of ascendancy over another. They do not cherish the thought of being better than the other person, nor do they thrive on the misfortunes of others. They want to be better, but better today than they were yesterday, and better tomorrow than they are today. They run their own race on their own track, remaining totally oblivious of the opinions of others. They are propelled into actions by motives which are noble, unadulterated by any wish or desire to deprive or cause pain to anyone.

There is a story of a twelve year-old boy, Toshi, who asked his parents for permission to run in the race on the sports day at school. His parent's reply was in the affirmative with a promise that they would attend the event. When the day arrived and it was time for his race, he stood at the starting point with other twelve year olds.

He was the tallest in the race, stood towering above all the contestants. The other parents there to support their sons noticed the unfair height advantage and supplicated Toshi was in a wrong age classification. They gave up all hopes of anyone else winning the race.

When the race started all the boys sprinted away leaving Toshi yards behind. Toshi ran as fast as he could but appeared to be struggling. Just then he looked at his father, with the eyes that said *'I have brought you shame'*. His father cried out *'Come on, Toshi, you can do it'*. By now the race was nearly over, but his parents continued to exhort him to run. Seeing this all other parents joined them in urging Toshi to run. All the boys who had crossed the finish line heard the crowd cheering Toshi. They turned round and joined the chorus. The entire field clapped their hands as the lone figure approached the finish line, and there was a deafening roar as Toshi finished the race.

It emerged later, when a special announcement was made, that Toshi had limited lung capacity and was somewhat incapable of leading the physical life of a standard twelve year-old child. He was commended for setting an example to all other children that seemingly impossible tasks are not out of reach simply because others have chosen to put limits on us.

You see, he was running a different race, his own, and it did not matter who crossed the line first. Toshi's real purpose was to prove to his parents that he was not incapable despite his incapacity.

Tiger Woods, the legendary golfer, is a fine example of an individual who is one in a million rather than one of a million, not because he is such a great golfer, but because he has been able to gain the attention of people all around the world who will him to do well and win. Spectators and commentators who watch him play, those who watch him on live television, those who read about him in the newspapers, even those who do not know the first thing about golf, would like to know how he is faring. They all carry a desire to see him win.

This is because he has lit a new torch of hope for those of us mere mortals who have been conditioned to accept limitations imposed upon us by our social environment, where history and records that tell us that we are incapable of achieving greater feats in any field of endeavour. Tiger inspires the younger generations to strive for the impossible. His steadfast devotion to his craft, relentless strife for excellence in all circumstances and intense application of mind to purpose at hand are hallmarks of a veritable winner. His actions tell any young aspirant that continued success is possible with the cultivation of these qualities and it does not come by chance or luck but by devotion, perseverance and pursuit. When we take a firm grasp of these disciplines, we begin to gain the realisation that we are the masters of our destinies. Tiger sets out not necessarily just to win, but also to set new and higher standards that expose unexplored human capabilities.

Tiger's open display of gratitude and respect for his parents is symbolic of an upbringing given by a loving and caring family. His qualities and achievements are truly inspirational to others. His actions are no less, for he is also putting back into the world what he has gained from it; his Centre For Learning in Southern California, set up for young aspiring children, built to provide skills and knowledge desired by the children themselves, is a fine example of a person living his purpose.

To run our own race means living our purpose which is the most natural thing to do. But to discover our natural purpose we need to set aside all the clutter of years of conditioning and scripting etched on us by our surrounding. As we clear the clutter, we pave the way for a journey within which opens up vast unbounded spaces for our spirit to soar and reach unimaginable heights. This race is not about speed, but patience; not about flight, but faith; not about ascendancy over others, but integrity with others; not about superiority over others, but purity of purpose; not victory over others, but mastery over self, and most of all, it is not about leaving others behind, but about leading a unique path.

3

"No-one Owes You a Favour"

This principle is based on another fundamental understanding that selfless and unconditional giving is the primal intent of the Universal Force.

The universe has to be mirrored in each of us who seeks a harmonious existence with it. Life itself is a very serious business ('busy-ness'). There is so much going on inside each living body which is shedding dead cells and creating new ones every second of our existence. All our organs are replaced in a set cycle and this is taken for granted so much that we do not even realise this perpetual miracle at the core of our existence. We do not keep a record of what Nature is continually giving us.

To be one with Nature and to mirror it, I have to make giving second nature to me, and keep no record or memory of it. I heard a business owner once talking to his friend on the phone. This friend was in some kind of difficulty and wanted the business owner to talk to a mutual acquaintance on his behalf. The businessman gave assurance that he would talk to them and definitely resolve the problem because he said, *"he owes me a favour"*. I was a little perplexed by those words.

How can anyone owe you a favour? If you have done someone a favour, it is an act of giving on your part. And as it is a favour, it has to be selfless, charitable and humane. It is unconditional; there cannot be an expectation of a similar act in return. There cannot be a record or treasured memory of this act on the part of the giver. True charity is when the act is done and nothing is said thereafter by the benefactor. If that is not the case, the act becomes a business transaction. The receiver of the favour becomes indebted and the giver carries the burden of collecting. Both are under stress. This works in total conflict with the intent of Nature, and if extended to the entire human race, organised social order would disintegrate.

Therefore, someone *owing you a favour* is warped thinking, as its total application to all human beings leads to harmonious life not being possible.

Equally too much eagerness to reciprocate or return an act of favour, to 'square up the score' as it were, is a form of ingratitude. In selfless giving a true giver experiences a veritable joy, not dissimilar to that which the deserving recipient experiences. To deny someone such joy is in itself an act of ingratitude and a show of arrogance.

All known religions are founded on charity as one of their precepts. The beauty of selfless giving is that it makes the recipients feel worthy, recognised and the givers good about themselves. The recipients remain in a state of gratitude and instinctively become givers in their own right. And if they are givers, then in this continuum givers have to be recipients at some stage! If someone gives me a gracious or out of gratitude gift, I will choose to accept it, even if it is of no use to me. I will then seek someone who can benefit from it, and pass on the gift to that person. It makes me morally enriched and strong, and never poorer or deprived. You see, in the words of J C Maxwell, evangelical Christian author, speaker, and pastor, *'your candle loses nothing when it lights another candle'*.

True giving has to be unconditional; otherwise it becomes a transaction which needs to be balanced by an act of reciprocation. If reciprocation does not come, imbalance, conflict and dissatisfaction ensues. The result of this is despair and loss of desire to do any more of the so-called favours. I have known many people say something like, *"You do so much for others, but you never get appreciation for it. All you get in return is ingratitude. From now on no more favours, no more giving."*

This kind of culture is contradictory to what Mother

Teresa's most inspiring poem entitled *Anyway* says for selfless giving.

> *People are often unreasonable, illogical and self centered*
> *Forgive them anyway.*

> *If you are kind, people may accuse you of selfish, ulterior motives;*
> *Be kind anyway.*

> *If you are successful, you will win some false friends and some*
> *true enemies;*
> *Succeed anyway.*

> *If you are honest and frank, people may cheat you;*
> *Be honest and frank anyway.*

> *What you spend years building, someone could destroy overnight;*
> *Build anyway.*

> *If you find serenity and happiness, they may be jealous;*
> *Be happy anyway.*

> *The good you do today, people will often forget tomorrow;*
> *Do good anyway.*

> *Give the world the best you have, and it may never be enough;*
> *Give the world the best you've got anyway.*

> *You see, in the final analysis, it is between you and your God;*
> *It was never between you and them anyway.*

There is story of a beggar who went round all day about his begging business, and returned to his ramshackle dwelling under a bridge over a small stream in a busy city. As he sat down to have his meal, he saw his mate lying down barely covered by a tattered blanket, and asked him, *"What kind of day have you had?" "I haven't*

been out today, I have a fever and I am feeling very cold" was
the reply. On hearing this the first beggar, without a
second thought, relinquished his claim on his meal and
gracefully placed it beside his friend, saying, "Have this,
and don't worry. I will be back just now." He went to a
drug store and spent all his day's alms to buy medicine
for his friend. He himself drank water that night and
slept peacefully. That night he gave away all he had for
the well-being of another. Even a beggar can be a
magnificent giver. Giving is not the domain of the
wealthy only.

George Bernard Shaw, playwright and critic, sums
up the life of giving in his mission statement:

> 'This is the true joy in life - being used for a purpose
> recognised by yourself as a mighty one, being a true force
> of nature instead of a feverish, selfish little clod of
> ailments and grievances complaining that the world will
> not devote itself to making you happy. I am of the opinion
> that my life belongs to the whole community, and for as
> long as I live, it is my privilege to do for it whatever I can. I
> want to be thoroughly used up when I die, for the harder I
> work the more I live. I rejoice in life for its own sake. Life is
> no brief candle to me. It's a sort of splendid torch which
> I've got to hold up for the moment, and I want to make it
> burn as brightly as possible before handing it on to future
> generations.'

Selfless giving produces a mood-lifting substance called serotonin in the brain of the giver. Serotonin creates a state of 'feeling good' about oneself. Anyone can create such a state about themself. You do not have to be rich to give. I can choose to give friendship, time, unconditional love, teach someone a skill I possess or pass on knowledge. You see the most precious gifts are not tangible or expensive, and most of all, they are not favours, merely evidence of dedication to being used for a mighty purpose.

4

"THE REAL ENEMY IS WITHIN"

This principle is at the heart of everything that I experience. If I am the effect of everything that happens around me, and if I wish to be the cause of everything that I experience, what is stopping me?

It is a myth for me to believe that any force that stops me from being proactive or taking responsibility for my state is outside of me. The secret of individuals who have the penchant for eternally joyful existence and who appear to be living in total harmony with their entire surrounding, is simply knowing that all hindrances to whatever they wish to attain are inside them, is in the way they process information and react to events taking place around them. Their thinking process, and hence growth and happiness, is not adulterated by the presence of the five dominating passions which lurk within each one of us. These passions - lust, anger, greed, attachment and vanity - are the real enemy within.

Lust is the first one. It is commonly misunderstood as an extreme desire for sexual gratification but in a spiritual context this most natural of instincts is only lust when this act is performed for the selfish fulfilment of one against the will of the other or to the detriment of the other. Sexual molestation is definitely lust and also any other perverse sexual act. Sex used in its legitimate purpose is an extreme expression of love.

But lust goes beyond sexual acts. Any extreme, abnormal and obsessive indulgence in wealth accumulation, drugs, alcohol, exotic foods, tobacco, obscene literature, entertainment such as gambling and winning at any cost would all be classified as lust. This is when a normal function of the mind is let to regress into abnormality. In this state an individual ceases to care for common decency, health, safety, welfare of others or any consequences of his or her actions.

In business he can be so obsessed with enhancing profit that without any hesitation or compassion he will condemn as useless and ruthlessly dismiss employees if there is a slightest threat to profits. Removal of all opposition to remain at the helm of a political office through misuse of power by a leader is also a form of lust. Ruthless and frenzied slaughter of human beings simply because they are of a different ethnic group is the worst form of lust. Extreme lust puts a man on the lowest rung of the ladder of all living creatures.

Anger is another passion which can be very destructive. It manifests itself in a number of subtle ways. It is not only a strong feeling of annoyance, displeasure or hostility, but also a state of frustration, impatience, indifference or intolerance. It manifests itself most commonly in the form of jealousy, envy, gossip, nagging, extreme criticism and all kinds of non-complimentary remarks directed at others or self. It lurks in all of us in different guises.

Nagging one's spouse or comparing with others to make them feel wanting in some respect, demonstrating dissatisfaction or frustration through fault-finding or spending a lifetime trying to change another person, showing callous disregard or indifference, calling people by derogatory names and even maliciously damaging property or telling blatant lies are all forms of anger. This is a core disease which even the most gifted of medics cannot cure, and is the cause of a great many failings and much unhappiness amongst people.

Greed, also known as avarice or covetousness, is another devastating passion. An intense and selfish desire for disproportionate wealth, power, food, fame or any recognition, ignoring the realm of the spiritual, is greed. A greedy person is self-serving and highly consumed with materialistic ambitions and is divorced from the notion of a humane society. Such a person lives under a constant scarcity mentality and may serve personal interest - even at the expense of others.

Greed can drive a person to all lengths to gratify acquisitive instincts. They will place self-interest, property and material before family and friends, and can go to the extent of breaking relationships and tell lies to preserve personal interest. Greed is not simply in the domain of the wealthy. A wealthy person will make a large donation in public and seek recognition of it, whereas someone who is not wealthy will make a donation and seek recognition for it, each expecting a return from a donation.

Greed is pernicious as it corrupts people of all ages in all walks of life. An individual donating a large sum of money to a political party in return for a favour, a pharmaceutical company paying a research analyst a disproportionate sum of money to write a favourable report on a new drug to promote it, a retail shop owner unscrupulously removing cash out of the till and understating his earnings to the taxman, a customs official taking a bribe to let a consignment of prohibited narcotics in to a country and so on, are all forms of greed that erode fundamentally.

Greed resides at the centre of any culture of bribery and corruption. Greed to accumulate wealth and achieve reputation from position of privilege and trust such as in the financial industry can lead individuals into compromising accepted standards of decent behaviour and putting in jeopardy whole industries and economic systems. When a large group of individuals is consumed by greed, the outcome can be devastating for a whole nation.

Say a politician, wishing to gain political power, promises to reduce taxes. Masses vote him and his party into office and, sure enough, the promise to cut taxes is kept. Ultimately, in order to balance the books, government expenditure is cut in the maintenance of hospitals, prisons and schools. The result is that doctors become indifferent as there are no beds to offer to people suffering from serious mental disorder who are therefore let loose in the community; and if prison security is compromised on account of budgetary constraints, drugs can find their way into prisons or convicts can escape. If schools cannot buy sufficient books or recruit better qualified teachers, education suffers with a lasting effect on the whole nation's future.

Attachment to material objects, an ideology, identity, position, people, work and anything of that nature is another passion which lurks in us in such a subtle form that we do not even recognise that it has put gripping shackles on our minds. It stops us from reaching out and growing spiritually because we are made to remain in fear of losing what we possess, not knowing that we can cultivate a state of the mind which claims ownership of the entire universe and yet possesses nothing – not even ourselves.

Attachment, or fear of losing something, takes a toll on our natural talents and brings much strife, stress and turmoil in our lives. Our house becomes our castle and we spend endless hours over-protecting it and its contents by installing double locks, a burglar-proof security system and then insuring it all. We acquire tasteful furniture and then make rules about its usage such that our own children feel stifled in the home and visitors feel uneasy as our guests. We preserve clothes and ornaments we do not really need and allow them to occupy space that we are forced to create. Our status at work becomes an important source of our reputation and power such that we live in constant fear of losing it. We resist telling others how we do our work for fear of being replaced. We are born in a religious faith and brought up in it such that we call it our religion and are willing to die for it, as if it needed protecting.

Our possessiveness towards our accumulations and reputation adds physical and mental clutter to our lives and builds prison-walls around us.

Vanity is the fifth and, at its extreme end, the deadliest of the passions. It is a state of self-deception and delusion that we find ourselves in as we gain worldly education and grow and prosper. We acquire a false sense of individuality. We begin to measure ourselves against the others around us, compare our appearance, accumulations and achievements with theirs and look for ways to see ourselves as separate and superior beings.

If we do not succeed in this regard, we seek to

distinguish ourselves by trying to be culturally superior or by claiming our ancestry as having evolved from some reputable historical background. In some instances we make a brief encounter, direct or indirect, with a renowned person our claim to fame. We somehow want to portray ourselves as wealthy or superior or more accomplished, and this becomes the only means of feeling good about ourselves.

The underlying emotions in this kind of behaviour are fear, insecurity and inadequate self-worth. Such individuals generally lack the understanding of life at a deeper level and so every thought they express lacks the force of energy. They live in a world of make-believe.

This ultimately crumbles to expose the true reality. To such people that which is seen is more real than that which is invisible. Looks and appearance matter more than character and values, and looking young through surgery and make-up matters more than the underlying health of the body and mind. Such individuals are not themselves. They live a life of pretence and bask momentarily in the illusory world they create around themselves. They are so insecure that they have to put up a defensive front. Their soul depends on the nourishment from the good opinions about them expressed by others.

A river in monsoon looks at itself and revels in the grandeur of its expanse. It is flanked by overflowing banks on either side; its depth concealed in its silent blue colour depicts its power which can bring down bridges and carry the weight of mighty ships. Nothing stands in its way. As it flows for miles, lapping up every obstacle in its way, it gains a regal sense of invincibility, only to be humbled when it reaches the sea which engulfs it without a murmur. In a similar vein, vanity gives one a false impression about oneself, ultimately for one to only discover that there is a truly great and veritable force of nature which reminds one that, in the grand and infinite scheme of existence, individuals come and go like the particles of dust in a beam of sunlight penetrating a tiny air vent in the wall. Vanity puts a mask on reality.

Our false self-portrait is constituted by these passions in varying degrees. Their only purpose is to create an illusory world which shields us from experiencing the joy of being connected vibrationally to the universal source of our being.

5

"YOUR RESOLUTIONS ARE SACROSANCT"

The understanding of this principle is crucial for me if I have to succeed in fulfilling all my intentions. The emphasis here is on 'your', meaning one's own personal and very close to heart. The term 'sacrosanct' here means deserving to be treated with seriousness and respect and as divine. Resolutions are the statements of intent seated deep in the core of one's heart.

Every genuine resolution is the result of an intense dialogue with one's inner-self to bring about a positive and meaningful change in one's life. Resolutions are powerful statements of intent we make to ourselves. They are promises we make to ourselves. They can be vows taken to behave or act in certain ways. I have found that true resolutions are borne out of an intense desire to attain something following an emotional experience. Every thought we have is a form of powerful energy which becomes a desire or intent. But for a desire or intent to be manifested into reality, it has to be matched by an equal, concentrated and consistent level of energy.

Such energy is successfully created by meditating or

contemplating. If a desire is pronounced glibly and announced openly to all and sundry by a spoken word, the level of energy in it becomes less. When we speak to others, who are not our closely loved ones, and share with them our deep emotions, we expect them to share with us the weight of these matters. This process of sharing takes our attention to their reaction, and so the energy is dissipated. Thus the strength of desire, confidence in expectation and courage to act are weakened.

That is why a personal resolution must remain as an inner dialogue with the self so the energy contained in it is not dissipated. A personal resolution is meant to bring a desired outcome, a habitual change or an improvement in behaviour. It is personal, but it may be to influence the outside world.

Some types of resolution can be to give up smoking or drinking, reduce weight and improve health through diet control and exercise, desist from malicious gossiping, strive to see good in all, avoid being perpetually negative, eradicate prejudice, work harder, donate to good causes, avoid conflict or vehement disagreement and seek peace when there is choice.

We all make resolutions to improve ourselves, our self- image and circumstances to bring happiness into our lives. A personal resolution is very much a part of oneself, having taken birth from deep within, and has to be treated as sacrosanct. It is not forced on you by another person, because if it is, it ceases to be personal and lacks the energy to be effective. And that is why vows taken during a marriage ceremony, which are dictated by the presider of the ceremony, do not always produce lasting results, but two individuals can bring about a lasting relationship if they constantly make spontaneous declarations, promises and pledges to each other from within. There is immense energy and invincible determination in such undertakings which are born from deep within. Being born from there, they originate from an esoteric source which is what makes them sacrosanct.

6

"DEATH IS NOT A PUNISHMENT"

I begin with the words of J. Krishnamurti: *"Death must be something extraordinary. Life is a total thing - sorrow, pain, anguish, joy, absurd ideas, possessions, envy, love, the aching misery of loneliness – all that is life. And to understand death, we must understand the whole of life, not take just one fragment of it and live with that fragment, as most of us do. In the very understanding of life - there is the understanding of death, because the two are not separate."*

I affirm that death is not an end of existence. Death is an integral part of the physical life. The physical is a field of duality in which as there is death so there is life. Without death, life would not be; just as without darkness, light would not be and without winter, summer would not be. Nature's inexhaustible agenda is to create, maintain and destroy in a continuum. I am a product of Its processes and there is no escape from Its programme.

Accepting death as inevitable adds meaning and greater purpose to physical life. I want to live every pulsating moment to the fullest and have no fear of dying. Living to the fullest to me means immersing myself in all the wonderful and bewildering mysteries of life, accepting what comes my way as an intent or gift of Nature, making my own weather, thus eliminating the need to complain about heat or cold, accepting natural diseases as natural and seeking Nature's intervention which can come in all kinds of guises, eliminating debilitating passions like lust, anger, greed, attachment and vanity and living in a state of gratitude for each dawn that awakens me.

People fear death because they are afraid of the unknown, but then how much do we know about life? How well do we live amongst ourselves? Why do we not respect life? We live in daily strife, squabbles and major conflicts. If we believe life is all there is with nothing thereafter upon death, why do we not live it to the fullest?

We think of and live in the past. We are seeking something permanent whilst in an impermanent life state, and the only thing solid we know is our past. But living in the past is only a recipe for not letting old wounds heal or rejecting the present in favour of the past, thus showing discontent with the present. Living in the past is a lazy mind's non-acceptance of the inevitable. Such a mind does not live life to the fullest.

Fear of death exists in many minds because we have been told about punishments of 'burning in hell' by the propagators of 'laws of God' who want to impose their will on weak minds and deter them from committing what are described as sinful acts in society.

The death penalty for certain crimes in many parts of the world has also contributed to death as being fearful. I only say to myself that as I have no recollection at present of any experience of what happens after life, I choose to go by the more plausible law of retribution, or cause and effect, or action and reaction. Nature is a super-intelligent power that has created a perfectly balanced universe that I am able to see and experience.

Under the law of retribution, each soul seeks perfection and until it has reached this state, it returns to earth through rebirth in order to redress the imbalance it has created through its actions or inactions. When a soul has redressed itself, it becomes ready to dwell on the higher spiritual planes, its natural abode, as a co-worker with Nature, words written by Pierre Teilhard de Chardin, a French visionary Jesuit, *'we are not human beings having a spiritual experience, but spiritual beings having a human experience'* being most appropriate.

I am carrying an aspect of the Higher Force and my destiny is to return to It - my natural habitat in the cosmic world, and so when I die there will be no burning in hell; I will either be retained or return to physical existence. I live in no fear of punishment for I seek the balanced existence in which I have no guilt.

I learnt from my mother how acceptance of the inevitable can add joy and substance to one's life. She taught me that natural death is an event one can look forward to without any fear; dying is an art. I once asked her in a jocular fashion at a family gathering, "*…you are now an old woman, you sit all day with little to do. What are you living for?" She replied, "When I see you all, your spouses, your children and your grandchildren, all thirty-four of you, then my heart fills with deep joy. And I look forward to the day when I will meet your father in heaven and say to him 'You left me with six young children. I raised them and gave them nurture as best as I could. They and their families are all well and have prospered. I have fulfilled my task' I rise each morning and contemplate this moment. It fills my day."* The strength of her words and certitude in her statement are lost in this translation into English.

I was fortunate enough to have been with her during her last few days and at her bedside, along with several others from our family, during her final moments as her soul was departing. I have yet to see a more peaceful and serene face as I did on that night. She was at total peace with herself, appeared to have been looking forward to her death and to my complete amazement her face actually looked a little younger. The whole episode was as if she had switched herself off. It was her wish that her going should not be mourned, but rather be a private occasion to celebrate her life.

The real fear in me is not of dying but of how I am going to die and what mess I am going to leave behind for others to clear. I deserve no punishment if I live knowing that I am guided by the Higher Force that fills me with thoughts, emotions, words and actions and I seek to become the instrument of Its purpose, and thus have no sense of guilt.

To me death is no punishment, but rather an opportunity - since under the law of retribution I will either return to another life in human form or become a co-worker with the Higher Force of Nature – and if I am to return, I may as well start to think about my next life now, so I can avoid all the pitfalls and frailties of human existence and look forward to the wondrous offerings of life on earth which have eluded me in this lifetime.

7

"YOUR CHILDREN ARE NOT YOURS"

This belief statement emerges from the principle that death is not a punishment, and that our permanent form is spiritual in a domain which is non-physical and without time and space.

As I think about this principle and begin to espouse it, I find that I am becoming emotionally free - that does not mean free of emotions – but rather I understand my soul and seek to free it from melodrama. Thus I strive to be free of malice, resentment, strong opinions, emotional ties, self importance and any other kind of ego-gratifying emotion. I am part of the universal whole and the universal whole is me, thus there is total unity or non-duality – there is no 'me' or 'mine'. As a parent I do not have to own my children nor do I have to strive to create my own protégés.

Parents are the first school where life's teachings begin, and true teachings must be enlightening, empowering and inspiring for the child to exploit the naturally gifted intellectual capacity and inquisitiveness for life's mysteries – neither inhibiting nor exploitative for the selfish motives of the parents.

My natural inclination from the time I began to become aware of myself, was to break from all social conditioning and split from any form of attachment that I found to be confining, restrictive and hindering my aim to be free flowing and independent in my thinking. This desire was allowed not to be frustrated by my mother and my elder brother, neither of whom ever made any restrictive rules when it came to religion, race, creed, colour or nationality, nor did they see the need for any venture-inhibiting family rules of any kind. Thus I had no ideological shackles put on me at home, nor was anyone too protective of me or fearful that harm may come to me.

It was this environment that gave me a fearless and unbounded mind and yet there was a bondage that kept us all together in spirit. Somehow I felt unfettered, unstifled and yet very close to my mother and my brothers and sisters. There was no compulsion to continue in any rigid family tradition. I consider myself to be most fortunate to have been raised in such a family environment that was conducive to growth of free thought that enabled cultivation of skills to give appropriate responses to varying challenges in life and to build my principles and values.

Thus I learnt to 'fish the stream', as it were, or to know my economic, social, psychological and spiritual environments for my nurturance, growth and survival. The most important thing was to seek harmonious co-existence with my environment. 'Harmonious' and 'Co-existence' are the two guiding magic words which are key to successfully meeting all challenges which threaten livelihood and life itself. Any parents who teach their children how to survive enjoy relief at the deepest level and freedom from attachment and anxiety. Their children are taught primary considerations in life.

These fundamental teachings focus on substance or character rather than exterior appearance or personality of a subject – less form and more formless. Their basic guidance comes from an internal reference point – they are less reliant on others to constantly lead them, hold their hand and give them a secure shelter. They can survive without their parents, and their parents do not see compulsion to remain attached to their children for their security in old age. Such parents do not let the love for their children impair their understanding of the life continuum and true purpose of life at a spiritual level, and weaken their sense of existence. Life goes on under the auspices of the Creator who loves all Its creations more than do those instruments that serve the purpose of bringing life forth.

The poem written by Kahlil Gibran in The Prophet poignantly encapsulates this thought and affirms this basic truth I espouse:

> *Your children are not your children.*
> *They are the sons and daughters of life's longing for itself.*
> *They come through you, but not for you.*
> *And although they are with you, they belong not to you.*
> *You may give them your love, but not your thoughts.*

For they have their own thoughts.

You may house their bodies, but not their souls.

For their souls dwell in the house of tomorrow,

which you cannot visit, not even in your dreams.

You may strive to be like them, but seek not to make
them like you.

For life goes not backward, nor tarries with yesterday.

You are the bows from which your children as living
arrows are sent forth.

The Archer sees the mark upon the path of the infinite,

and He bends you with His might that his arrows may go
swift and far.

Let your bending in the Archer's hand be for gladness.

For even as He loves the arrow that flies, so He loves the
bow that is stable.

8

"YOUR WEALTH IS MY JOY"

At the highest level of existence – the level of total integrity or complete oneness – I experience myself living in one overarching energy field. At this level I see myself in all, and all in me. This state of being is the key to making life joyful.

It has the potential to liberate one from the grips of harmful emotions like greed for massive material accumulations and power over others. It also overcomes jealousy, envy, frustration, bitterness, ill-will, resentment and despondency, which are all subtle forms of anger prevalent in the modern times of highly polarised and stratified communities with increasingly widening gap between the haves and the have-littles. This is the level of boundless horizon from where I see myself claiming ownership to everything I can visualise and therefore see no need to possess anything.

Whilst there is an increasing level of literacy and material comforts, there is an equally increasing level of discord, disillusionment and unrest, all born out of greed for more and attachment to material possessions.

My disillusionment with the common mistaken understanding of wealth has given rise to this principle in my working creed. All around me I mostly see nothing but strife to acquire, accumulate and retain money and physical assets misconstrued as wealth and far less concern for creation and preservation of real wealth. There is far too much misconception about wealth and what it can do for its owner.

For a start the worth of a person's wealth is measured by the value put on his or her possessions by market forces and opinions. How much such wealth an individual owns determines the level of his or her success in life and standing in society and this measure is one significant criterion, if not the only one, that most people will consider to figure out if an individual has attained anything in life. It is fervently believed that this kind of wealth gives power and respect in society. It makes it possible to open most doors in life. It is the gateway to bliss.

Whilst it is necessary to live well, support all dependents and provide for retirement, man's obsession with this idea has placed him on a merry go round of limitless possessions. His penchant for possession has blinkered him as he relentlessly strives towards ownership, rather than stewardship, of even larger swathes of the natural gift to mankind - the planet Earth. His unceasing pursuit of ownership of land for his security demonstrates how narrow-minded and misguided he has become in his absurd and futile pursuit of this alien and fettering notion; he has allowed himself to be selfishly attached to what he has not created, nor can take anywhere with him, yet he craves for more and more possession of it. One only needs to see how much strife is brought about from wars fought over land.

Money is used as a commodity to derive vast fortunes from money itself without producing anything tangible. Families and nations fall out with differences over wealth. The crass self-centredness and indifference is endemic to human nature. The evident state of the disappearing habitable environment and disequilibrium in the distribution of wealth is testimony to it. The present day deep international economic crisis that has arisen from greed-inspired behaviour of unprincipled individuals in financial institutions has created a mountain of trillions of dollars of toxic assets which can only be described as the value of food that has been snatched from the mouths of hungry children of the future.

It was a comment made to me by a one-time school friend that truly got me thinking in this direction. This friend, whom I knew very well as a teenager, invited me to his house one day for old times' sake. He was really keen to tell me how well he had done in life. I learnt from him how he had accumulated a portfolio of acres of land and a number of properties, how his family and community were proud of him and how much respect he was enjoying from people who knew him. I sensed arrogance and apathy on his part towards family, friends, relations and people in general. After much boasting he said he needed help to better manage his affairs and enquired if I would be willing to carry out some assignments for him. I replied in the affirmative. He proceeded to unfold his personal wealth statement to me.

I expressed my genuine appreciation of his accomplishments in a dignified manner, taking care not to sound sycophantic. However, my staid response did not appear to go down well with him. I suspect he was expecting me to react like a servile flatterer, only too willing to serve him. I guess that was his definition of respect. He finally said rather sternly, *"Whilst I am proposing that you carry out assignments for me for a fee and whilst I have disclosed in confidence to you the full extent of my wealth, I expect you not to cast your beady eyes on my assets. These are my hard earned accumulations and I have no intention of sharing them with anyone"*.

He must have thought that I may demand a stake in his estate in return for services. He sounded like a boy telling other kids to keep their hands off his toys. I was stunned but chose not to react to his demeaning statement. My further meetings with him to discuss the nature of my involvement in his affairs revealed there was too much discord in his life. He was involved in a number of business cases of dispute and litigation, the true gravity of which he had concealed from his family.

Whilst he had accumulated a number of properties, some of his actions were being questioned. He was rapidly losing credibility, his relationships were failing and he was fast becoming isolated, even from his close relatives. I could not really help him and frankly did not feel comfortable in this relationship. I found good reasons for not being able to spare the time. Thus we drifted apart and I did not see him again. I failed to derive any joy from his so called wealth as he was overwhelmed by the need to survive the pressures mounting on him from all directions. He was not a happy man and hardly enjoyed being rich.

Sadly he passed away suddenly one day. I thought to myself, '*there is no wealth greater than the natural gift to live a life in a state of detachment as free of stress as possible. An immense amount of strife and tension can be alleviated if people do not have to be obsessed with the idea of amassing material assets and then striving to secure them from being taken away or plundered and pillaged.*'

This principle is the key to solving great many conflicts. These are conflicts inside us – for example, the clash of emotion and ideology. Emotion may dictate need for wealth because wealth is seen as a panacea for all misery and ideology may say money is not everything – it is evil. Jealousy and frustration may lead one to say unkind things about the wealthy. From observing behaviours of different people and reflecting on my own state of consciousness from my youthful years, I realised how people despise and envy those who are fortunate enough to have amassed material wealth and so do not have to endure the daily grind of having to make a mere living, and at the other end of the spectrum how many people with wealth become selfish and indifferent.

Why are so many wealthy individuals hated or loathed? Why do people have a cynical attitude towards them? Why do people not have goodwill towards them? Why is it not common to witness anyone experience a joyful feeling when they hear about or meet a wealthy person?

I strive hard to work towards consummate adoption of this principle and to deeply internalise it so as to be fully entrained and synchronised with it. All the assimilated habits of thought have to be slowly and systematically unlearned. I have to remind myself, not only to set aside, but seek to eliminate any thoughts of unfairness in any perceived unequal distribution of wealth. Any expression of unfairness or despondency or feeling of being deprived means very simply disconnecting myself from and cursing the force of Nature – being immobilised. At the other end of the scale, feeling and expression of veritable joy are spiritually uplifting, empowering, liberating and, most of all, unifying. This then becomes a major step towards gaining mastery over self.

This poignantly simple, but undoubtedly idiosyncratic sounding idea that *'what is not mine gives me joy'*, has forced me to question my pact with reality as I have known it for a large part of my life. It has forced me to seek true understanding of the purpose of life – which certainly is not being immobilised or imprisoned or possessed or enslaved, but is, as in the words of a Hindu saint, *'to gain unitive awareness of God'*.

To grasp the notion of this principle, one has to be suited both temperamentally and in spirit; one has to transcend all limitations of the mind and become receptive to the state of all possibilities. One needs to broaden one's horizons unimaginably far so as to claim, in mind and spirit, ownership of the entire universe, and thus obliterate the need to possess or be attached to anything, knowing full well that all is there for the force of Nature to provide, and It determines who delivers it.

The principle seeks to promote understanding that ownership of wealth at a personal level is simply a notion but one can still live a balanced life with it. Adam

Smith, in his global description of wealth, calls it '*the annual produce of land and labour to satisfy human needs and wants, which helps to sustain and enrich life*'. Robert Kennedy called it '*things that make life worthwhile*'.

Ordinarily, wealth can mean abundance of items of economic value or controlling interest in them. But it can also be climate and natural beauty spots which are conducive to tourism bringing visitors, and thus livelihood, to a nation.

This principle seeks out, and is a tribute to, those who are truly wealthy. They are the chosen deliverers. In the context of this principle, wealthy are those who possess immense wealth together with the humane qualities of compassion and respect for others. They are humble and live in a constant state of gratitude to God for what they have. Being philanthropic, they derive their sense of achievement from being instrumental in improving the lives of others, which therefore includes me, and everyone's economic and social environment, which again includes me. They possess an abundance mentality – in their world there is no scarcity, nor is anything impossible, which means they live in a state of being aligned with the creative forces of Nature.

They are distinctive not by their possessions, but by their self-assuredness in whatever they do, which means they know whatever they desire is delivered. They begin their actions with the sense that the inner emotions speak louder than words as they patiently go about their business. They do not see individuals as lesser or greater than them, nor do they see all as equal – to them each individual is fascinatingly unique with notable qualities, which means they do not put them in packages of generalised descriptions.

Their sense of values is not determined by material achievements, but by their service orientation. They prefer to be used for mighty purposes, but do not seek glory or recognition for their deeds. They understand and are challenged by deprivation, poverty and social injustice, but are not emotionally weakened by it. Rather, they make it all theirs and as they do so, they begin to bring about positive changes. There is something regal about them.

I find it difficult not to experience joy in the presence of such individuals who exude positive energy that touches me. In this joyful state I become part of their world, I am in the embrace of their warmth and I cease to see myself as distinct from them. Any sense of deprivation falls by the wayside – what is theirs feels like mine, which means even their purpose becomes mine.

Now this rather oxymoronic sounding principle

becomes palatable to anyone who has never entertained a single thought along these lines. For me it has gone beyond a thought – it has been an ongoing endeavour to genuinely feel joy when I am close to someone who fits this description. This trait is one of the many significant building blocks of the process of realisation of mastery over my own-self. It prevents me from being consumed with rage, envy, bitterness and disappointment on seeing others supposedly better placed than myself. Instead, the opposite is true.

In presence of a genuinely wealthy person, with whom I have any kind of relationship or connection, I see myself as fortunately being within the energy field of someone who constantly lives in a joyful and self-reassured state of the mind founded on positive thoughts. Feeling joy in that moment has the effect of creating full harmonisation and entrainment with the consciousness of that individual. I am then welcomed into his or her world to enjoy the privilege of his or her hospitality. This is joy!

In this principle wealth includes rare and amazing talent, skill and capability to perform, good reputation based on the capacity to give or serve with kindness, attributes like trustworthiness, powerful wisdom and insights which can guide and influence communities and nations, power to heal others, goodwill of others, extraordinarily good health and all such positive attributes. Thus Mother Teresa was wealthy!